MUSIC TECHNOLOGY 101

INCLUDES VIDEO TUTORIALS!

BY HEATH JONES

ISBN 978-1-70511-027-0

Contact us:
Hal Leonard
7777 West Bluemound Road
Milwaukee, WI 53213
Email: info@halleonard.com

In Europe, contact:
Hal Leonard Europe Limited
42 Wigmore Street
Marylebone, London, W1U 2RN
Email: info@halleonardeurope.com

In Australia, contact:
Hal Leonard Australia Pty. Ltd.
4 Lentara Court
Cheltenham, Victoria, 3192 Australia
Email: info@halleonard.com.au

ACKNOWLEDGMENTS

I want to thank all of my mentors and colleagues who have supported, encouraged, and inspired me to be the best teacher that I can be. Specific thanks are extended to Wayne Langford for providing equal amounts of technology and music production expertise and support to get our program off of the ground. Thanks to Andrew Ratcliffe, John Snyder, and the folks at Tweed Studios in Athens, GA for freely offering their vast experience and expertise to genuinely support and promote music technology programs in our schools.

Thank you to the administration of Gwinnett Co. Public Schools for always making Fine Arts education a priority for our students, and specifically to the administration of McConnell Middle School for supporting and encouraging the growth of our music technology program.

Special thanks go to David Dover and Dr. Andy Edwards—great colleagues and even better friends—for their support and encouragement. They have always been there to offer advice and honest feedback. Music technology education will continue to grow in our state because of your work and leadership. Thanks also to my father-in-law, Dr. James Braswell, for being my editor-in-chief and proofreader.

Finally, I will forever be grateful to and dependent on the love and support of my family, parents, two awesome kids, and especially my best friend and wife, Jeanine.

CONTENTS

INTRODUCTION

In the interest of full disclosure, I am not an expert in music technology. I am not a recording or studio production guru. I wouldn't even be considered a technophile or technology enthusiast. I am a musician and teacher. After earning two degrees in music education, I spent 18 years as a high school and middle school band director. My move into the music technology lab was gradual and, at first, accidental, but it would soon become quite deliberate and incredibly rewarding. I share this in an attempt to quell the initial apprehension and feelings of inadequacy that you may have about teaching music technology.

I experienced the same feelings when I started. I learned through trial and error, hours spent surfing the internet, phone calls and lunch meetings with experienced colleagues, and by observing my students. I started with almost no experience using technology to create music. Since that time, I've been asked to serve on local and state-level committees to create music technology curriculum and standards, presented professional learning sessions at numerous state, regional, and national conferences, and started a website for music technology teachers with a worldwide audience. I'm as stunned about this as anyone! My point is that if I can do this, so can you!

One of the first tasks I was faced with was understanding exactly what it was that I was supposed to be teaching my students. Finding the answer to this question proved to be a challenge. I found that educators and professionals familiar with the recording and music industry tended to define a music technology curriculum in terms of the technology, equipment, and processes used in a recording studio. Some curricula focused on teaching students how to use recording equipment and manipulate technology but did little to teach them much about music. This is what I refer to as a music *technology* class. Further compounding the problem is the fact that teacher training programs in most colleges and universities are doing little to prepare music educators to teach music technology. If someone has a degree in music education, they've taken courses in how to teach wind instruments, string instruments, percussion, guitar, and piano, but they haven't been taught how to teach music technology as a creative art. There seems to be an unfortunate caste system in place where folk, popular, or commercial music is considered to be in the realm of informal music-making and shunned by most collegiate level schools of music that specialize only in formal music-making.

I believe that creating and producing music should be the foundation of every course that we teach. Unable to discover a source that could define what a music technology course is, I developed my own definition:

Music Technology is about using technology to create, capture, manipulate, and edit sounds to produce a final product that achieves specific artistic, expressive, and functional goals.

Music technology is not teaching anything through, or with, technology. We should not confuse a music technology course with a music theory/composition course that uses technology. Nor should we confuse it with a piano or guitar course that uses technology. The key point to remember here is that *technology is the musical instrument* that students will use to create and produce music. Of course, we have to teach them how to use the technology. The orchestra teacher must teach their students how to operate a violin, but the point of learning how to play a violin is not to simply be able to operate the instrument. The students are taught how to use the instrument(s) at their disposal to create and share music. At its most fundamental level, a music technology course should be about teaching students how to be creative, artistic, and expressive musicians.

My goal in writing this book is to provide practical, actionable, and easy-to-understand information, resources, and advice to anyone interested in teaching a music technology course or learning how to become a do-it-yourself music producer. Remember, if I can do this, so can you!

About the Video and Extra Content

To download or stream the supplemental video tutorials, visit *www.halleonard.com/mylibrary* and enter the code provided on page 1 of this book. A four-week classroom song project plan is also available for download (see Appendix A) in PDF format from this same location.

CHAPTER 1: THE MUSIC TECHNOLOGY LAB AND STUDIO

People will often contact me about starting a music technology program at their school. One of the first questions that they ask is, "What do I need to have in my lab and studio?" Understand that there is a difference between *wants* and *needs*. The reality is that you do not *need* much to get started. The only resource that I had when I started the music technology program at my school was a PC lab. I located as many online sources for free loops and sound generators that I could find for my students to use. Our only means of recording and editing was Audacity. It was not much, but it was enough to get my students creating music. As the program began, I shared student work with administrators and community partners while researching funding sources through local, regional, and national grant programs. Many public schools have access to funds designated for technology. The federal Every Child Succeeds Act created potential funding streams through Title I, II, and IV of the law that could be used to fund a music technology lab and equipment. I certainly do not recommend starting the way I did, but do not be discouraged from starting a program because you do not have the lab or resources that you *want*.

The Basic Lab

It is important to think about how to arrange the student and teacher workstations in the lab. The setup is going to drive how instruction is delivered, student learning is monitored, and support is provided to individual students. Some of these suggestions may seem obvious, but I have been in numerous music technology labs that were arranged so poorly that instruction and monitoring were severely affected.

The student workstations should be arranged so that the instructor can view all of the student computer monitors at the same time. There are some great apps and options available for screen sharing and remote monitoring of student computers, but these options take up space on the teacher or student's screen. By using a LCD projector connected to the teacher's computer, the students can see what is being demonstrated by the teacher without losing any available space on their computer screen (Figure 1.1). All of the students are facing the LCD screen at the front of the room. They just have to look up to see the screen without having to turn around or otherwise interrupt their workflow. The teacher is positioned behind the student workstations so all of the student computer screens can be seen in a glance from one position.

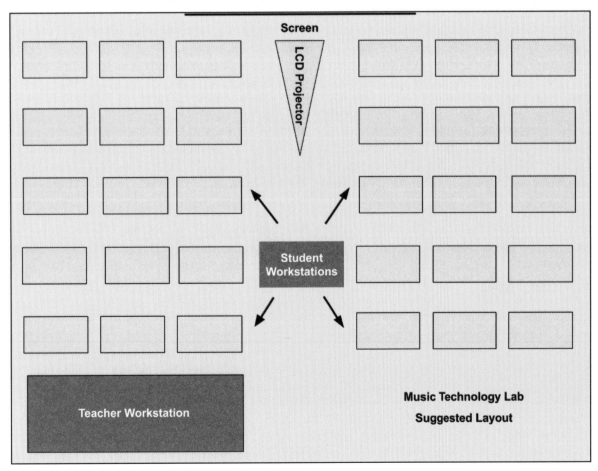

Figure 1.1

Another important consideration is the type of student desk that will be used. The initial lab and equipment may not include many peripheral devices, but that will change over time. *MIDI* (Musical Instrument Digital Interface) controllers—typically 25, 49, 61, or 88 keys—will be common in addition to other peripheral devices such as audio interfaces, fader ports, or pad controllers that may be added over time. Ideally, these should be organized as vertically as possible so the student does not have to turn away from the DAW to use these devices (Figure 1.2). This will also maximize the space available in the lab for your student workstations.

On-Stage Stands Workstation Desk
Figure 1.2

Once the lab space is planned and arranged, it's time to equip the student workstations. Each workstation should be equipped with a desktop or laptop computer. There are a few things to consider when choosing whether to use PC or Mac computers. The platform that is used will influence the software choices for the lab. Most of the available *DAW* (Digital Audio Workstation) programs on the market offer cross-platform compatibility, but a few do not.

Logic Pro is only compatible with Mac computers, while Mixcraft and Cakewalk are PC-compatible only. Also, consider file storage options and how that will work with the computer and software setup. iCloud storage will work great for Mac labs and Logic Pro or GarageBand files, but the Apple-based program files may not work well with Google Drive or other learning management systems such as Canvas, Blackboard, or Edmodo.

Headphones will be another essential item for the music tech lab. Two options are to either supply the headphones for the lab or require students to bring their own. Keep in mind that the lab is a teaching and learning space—not a dedicated professional studio. Professional-quality headphones are very expensive and will not be practical for most music tech lab applications. My advice with headphones is to use the cheapest over-ear headphones that you can find. Another consideration is whether or not a two-way communication system will be used in the lab. In this case, the headphones should also have a built-in microphone. If the lab is equipped with headphones, they will be getting a lot of use. The headphones will break and will have to be replaced. Expensive headphones could be a little more durable than the cheaper models, but not enough to justify the expense of replacing them when they break or wear out.

Bluetooth is the preferred method of connecting headphones to the computer. If Bluetooth is not an option, I highly advise that plugging headphones directly into the computer be prohibited. That connector will be an 1/8-inch jack which is notoriously fragile. Students plugging into an 1/8-inch jack on a daily basis will take its toll. A good solution would be to use an extension cable that stays plugged into the computer. Students can then plug into the extension (Figure 1.3). It's much easier and cheaper to replace an extension cable than it is to replace a broken headphone jack on the computer. Headphones can also be plugged into an audio interface. This is another good option if the interface uses a 1/4-inch jack. The 1/4-inch connector is much more durable than the 1/8-inch jack. A 1/8-inch to 1/4-inch converter is also a cheap accessory to make this arrangement work (Figure 1.4).

Figure 1.3

Figure 1.4

Next, consider what kind of device students will use to create or enter sounds into the DAW. A later chapter will go into more detail about the differences between creating and capturing sounds. This chapter will focus on the input device. A MIDI keyboard would be ideal for each workstation. There are some affordable models available, but purchasing a MIDI keyboard for each workstation is not essential. Most DAWs will allow students to create music in the DAW using the QWERTY keyboard that comes with the computer. MIDI mapping for QWERTY keyboards used as input devices for a DAW are generally universal (Figure 1.5).

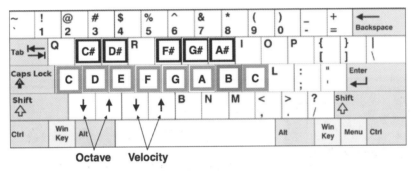

Figure 1.5

Using the QWERTY keyboard is not ideal, but it will work in a pinch. However, if MIDI controllers are beyond the budget for the music tech lab, I would place them at the top of the list for future upgrades. There are several models available that work well and cost less than $100, with some as low as $50 (Figure 1.6).

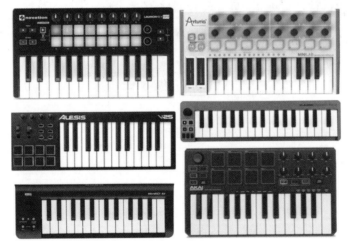

Figure 1.6

The teacher workstation is another important part of the music technology lab. This station should be equipped with the same peripherals and software of the student workstations, but with a few additional considerations. The teacher's computer should be connected to the LCD projector to display visual examples and demonstrations. It is not recommended that the sound is run through the same speakers as the projector. Investing in a pair of quality studio monitors is important for playback in the lab.

The final element of the basic music tech lab is the DAW software, which is used to create, record, edit, and produce music. Apple desktop and laptop computers come equipped with GarageBand installed. GarageBand is considered the "consumer" level DAW by Apple and is a great choice for beginner and novice level students. Logic Pro is considered the "professional" version of GarageBand and must be purchased separately. It's worth noting that GarageBand files created on a desktop or laptop do not transfer to GarageBand on the iPhone or iPad.

There are abundant reviews and descriptions of the most popular DAWs available on the market today. Soundtrap is a cloud-based DAW that offers some great features for a classroom setting. Because the platform is based in the cloud, Soundtrap works on any platform: Mac, PC, iOS, Android, etc. All that is needed is a web browser and access to the internet. This is a great feature if you have a Mac lab but the student has a PC at home or vice versa. A student can record into Soundtrap using a PC in the lab then switch to their iPad to edit and mix the project. Soundtrap also allows remote collaboration in real time. Collaborators can be invited into projects by the creator, and both can edit, mix, or add tracks in real time. Think Google Docs for music! A final feature for the classroom setting is that Soundtrap integrates with Google Classroom, Canvas, and several other learning management systems. The teacher can create a template in Soundtrap and then share the file as an assignment to the students. The collaboration button features an instant messaging window for the teacher to leave feedback and assess student work. Soundtrap is not as robust and full-featured as many other DAWs on the market for advanced music production, but is worth considering for a classroom setting.

The Advanced Lab

The next step to move the music tech lab beyond a basic setup is to add a *USB audio interface* to each student workstation. The audio interface translates audio signals into a digital format that the computer can use. Most audio interfaces will have connectors that allow inputs from 1/4-inch jacks as well as XLR connectors (Figure 1.7). The audio interface will greatly expand the input options available for the DAW.

Figure 1.7

The basic USB audio interface for home studio production or student work should have two input and two output channels. This will allow for stereo recording and playback. The XLR connectors would be most commonly used for studio microphones. The interface should be capable of supplying phantom power for any microphones that require external power. The 1/4-inch jack inputs will allow electric guitars, basses, and synthesizers to record directly into the DAW also. This is a great feature that allows creators to take advantage of the wide variety of amp simulators provided by most DAWs.

Monitoring student work and communication is another important consideration in the design of the music tech lab. The instructor needs to be able to hear what students are creating, and students should be able to share their music with the instructor and each other. Therefore, a key component of the music tech lab is a *modular communication system*. These systems connect the instructor to each student through a single interface. The instructor can have two-way communication with a single student, communicate with a select group of students, or with the entire class. Individual student work can be broadcast to the class either through headphones or monitors. These systems also have audio inputs at the teacher station to broadcast sound from external sources through monitors or the headphones at each student workstation.

Korg, Roland, and Yamaha each manufacture outstanding communication systems (Figure 1.8). The base systems will generally accommodate eight students and are expandable up to 48 students. The Korg and Yamaha systems also offer optional wireless control kits that enable the instructor to control the system with an iPad (not included with the system) from anywhere in the room. This is a great feature that frees the instructor from being tethered to the teacher workstation.

| Korg GEC5 | Roland GLC-1C | Yamaha LC4 |

Figure 1.8

The last piece of equipment to consider for a fully featured music tech lab is a quality pair of *studio monitors*. Some assume that a monitor is the same thing as a speaker, but there are significant differences. Speakers are generally designed for music consumers. The consumer is interested in the experience of listening to music. Consequently, speakers are designed to shape and color the sound output to create a pleasing sound for the consumer. Music is more portable today than it has ever been for music consumers. This has created a huge market for earbuds. Even more manipulation of the sound output is required in these products to create an acceptable listening experience for the consumer. Monitors, on the other hand, are designed specifically for the studio producer or engineer (Figure 1.9). A studio monitor generates a flat output without any added manipulation of the output frequencies or sound enhancements. This allows the music producer to hear a clean, unaltered version of the music playback as they make minute and detailed adjustments to the sounds being produced. Monitors are often designed to be listened to at close range. These are known as "near-field" monitors. While great for a small space or home studio, it is important to make sure that you get "far-field" monitors designed to broadcast to a larger space and audience. A trusted and experienced music retailer can help you choose and install an appropriate pair of monitors for your music tech lab.

Figure 1.9

The Extras

The equipment covered in this section can be acquired over time as resources allow. It will enable you to expand the curriculum, content, and experience that can be offered to students.

Recording live sound using microphones is an integral part of music technology. Most music tech lab rooms are less than ideal for recording live sound. Not only is the room itself not designed for recording, but creating a quiet environment can be difficult. Many products on the market can help mitigate these issues and improve the acoustic properties of the room.

Microphone shields can help reduce background noise and reduce the sonic ambience of a room (Figure 1.10). These devices are great for recording vocals, voice-overs, and *Foley* sounds (sound effects). While they do not provide sound isolation, they can greatly improve the quality of recorded audio.

sE Electronics

Primacoustic
Figure 1.10

Aston Microphones

Acoustic treatment can also be added to the walls of the room. These devices can be used to minimize the reverb and ambience of a room. Acoustic treatments either *absorb* or *diffuse* sounds. Absorption panels are usually flat, symmetrically shaped, made of soft materials, and help reduce the reflection of sound within a space. They can be hung onto the walls (Figure 1.11) or built into trap boxes that can be moved around a space or around instruments (Figure 1.12).

Figure 1.11

Primacoustic Trap Boxes
Figure 1.12

Large spaces with hard, parallel walls will benefit the most from absorption panels. Diffusion panels are usually curved or asymmetrically shaped and made from hard materials (Figure 1.13). Diffusion panels work to spread the sound evenly around a room to prevent "dead" or "live" spots. None of these devices can soundproof a room. Preventing sound from entering or leaving a space is a difficult proposition. There are some modular solutions available, but they can be expensive and require a space large enough to install the modules.

Primacoustic Diffusion
Figure 1.13

Once the room is treated, microphones are required to record live audio. There are abundant resources available that cover technical specifications and applications for the various types of microphones. The following section will focus on three broad categories of microphones that should be considered for outfitting the music tech lab.

XLR Microphones

The *XLR connector* (Figure 1.14) was developed in the mid-20th century by James H. Cannon and has been the standard connector for analog audio for over 50 years. *XLR microphones* utilize the XLR connector to connect to various kinds of analog audio equipment, including mixing boards, pre-amps, powered speakers, and PA systems. Using XLR microphones in the music tech lab will require an audio interface to translate the analog signal into a digital signal for the computer. Most of these audio interfaces require that a driver be installed on the computer. XLR mics are very versatile and can be used to record audio into a DAW via the audio interface, plugged into analog audio components, or used in live performance. XLR mic cables range in length from 1 to 100 feet. Music tech students need to be familiar with the applications of XLR microphones as well as how to connect these mics to various analog and digital components.

Figure 1.14

USB Microphones

USB microphones connect directly to the computer using a *USB cable* (Figure 1.15). The quality of USB microphones has increased tremendously since they were first introduced. Some now rival the sound quality of the best analog XLR microphones. USB microphones stand out for their ease of use. Most are "plug and play," meaning that no external audio interface is required for the computer to recognize the mic as an input source. The advantages of USB microphones must be considered against their considerable limitations in use. USB microphones are designed to work in a strictly digital environment and cannot be used with analog equipment. They are portable only to the degree that the computer they are connected to is portable. Most USB mic cables are 3 to 10 feet long. They tend to work pretty well as long as you are in the computer lab but can be limited for field recording or live sound applications.

Figure 1.15

Blue Yeti

Samson Meteor

Audio-Technica AT2020USB

Shure PG42

Samson Go Mic

Blue Snowball

Lightning Microphones

Lightning microphones make an excellent choice for highly mobile or personal recording and connect to iOS devices such as the iPhone, iPod, and iPad. Two companies in particular have developed some outstanding microphones that are highly mobile and flexible, notably the Zoom iQ6 (and iQ7) and the Shure MV88. A possible drawback for these microphones is Apple's decision to move to the Thunderbolt 3 connector for all of its newest mobile devices. There are Lightning-to-Thunderbolt 3 convertors available, however, until the microphone manufacturers develop Thunderbolt 3 compatible models.

Zoom iQ6

Zoom iQ7

Shure MV88

Lightning microphones typically record onto an app and require the transferring of the audio file from the device to the DAW. Nevertheless, the ability to capture high-quality audio with only an iPhone in your back pocket and one of these mics in your front pocket is fantastic.

Other MIDI Controllers

Using a mini MIDI keyboard controller is a great way to start, but having to rely on the octave controls to move up and down the range of the instrument can become tedious and cumbersome. Moving to a 49- or 61-key MIDI keyboard puts more sounds at your fingertips. Prices will change dramatically depending on whether or not the keyboard is strictly a MIDI controller or if it is also a synthesizer with a bank of sound samples.

Native Instruments Komplete Kontrol A49
(MIDI only) $225–$250 range

Yamaha MX 61 MIDI/Synthesizer
$750–$800 range

Another MIDI device to consider is a *pad controller*. While some mini MIDI keyboard controllers have integrated pads, they are usually limited to eight. Pad controllers can feel less intimidating to novice musicians than manipulating a keyboard and generally cost less than $100. AKAI makes a MIDI controller called the EWI Wind Controller, with models ranging from $300 to $800. The performer blows air into the EWI while manipulating the keys much like a clarinet or a saxophone. Tabletop or stand-mountable *drum pads*—that can be used with drum sticks for a more natural feel—range from $200–$1000+. MIDI-capable full-sized electronic drum kits are also available from $300–$2000+. And one of my personal favorites is the Jamstick MIDI controller, which looks like a weird little guitar and costs around $150–$200. This technology is constantly evolving. Any tool that can engage students in making music is a positive development.

Korg NanoPAD2

Yamaha Digital Drums

Alesis Electronic Drum Set

AKAI EWI Wind Controller

Jamstick+ 7 Fret MIDI Guitar

Jamstick Studio MIDI Guitar

CHAPTER 2: THE TOOLBOX

Once the music tech lab or home studio is designed and established, it's time to take a closer look at the individual workstation. Any creator—whether they're an artist or craftsman—must know what tools they have at their disposal and how to use them. The painter must know what brushes, paints, tools, and canvases they have at their disposal before creating the painting. Likewise, the digital musician must also understand what creative tools are at their disposal and be willing to explore and experiment with them in the creative process.

The vocabulary of the music technology world can be confusing. Much of this is due to how the worlds of music, technology, analog, and digital morphed together during the latter part of the 20th century. You'll see countless terms like audio, analog, digital, electronic, synthesizer, MIDI controller, sample, sampler, sampling, looping, sequencer, VST, editor, DAW, mixer, etc.; the list goes on. Many of these terms are incorrectly interchanged and often misunderstood. Understanding and using the correct terminology is important to learning how to create music with digital tools.

What Is Digital Technology?

How is sound defined in the world of music technology? Real sounds made by real instruments are referred to as *audio*. Acoustic instruments create audio, as do our voices and electronic instruments. An electric guitar is an acoustic instrument that uses electricity to amplify its sound, which is heard as audio through an amplifier. A synthesizer is an electronic instrument that creates or synthesizes sounds. Many of the instruments that we refer to as synthesizers today do not create or synthesize sound like the original instruments developed by the likes of Robert Moog or Don Buchla. Rather, they use audio samples programmed into the instrument and play them back as the keys are pressed.

What is meant by digital technology? A digit is a number. Computers use a binary coding language based on the numbers 1 and 0. Digital technology is referring to technology that processes this binary language. It requires electricity to operate, but not everything that uses electricity is digital. Digital audio is virtual, not real. A digital track doesn't contain any actual audio—just data that must be processed to create a sound. Analog recording is a process that converts sonic energy (vibration) into an electrical signal. That electrical signal is then either transferred to magnetic tape or used to etch grooves into a vinyl disc. Digital recording uses a process called *sampling* to store the audio signal. Essentially, it takes a snapshot (sample) of the audio wave over 44,000 times per second and then reconstructs the smooth audio wave from these stored points.

A MIDI controller does not create any sounds of its own. It's simply a tool used to enter instructions or data into a computer. MIDI instruments were developed to make this process of entering data seem more familiar and natural for musicians. The computer is not aware of the shape or design of the device sending the data. The familiar QWERTY keyboard could be referred to as an ADI (alphanumeric digital interface). The letters and numbers were organized this way because humans were already familiar with using a typewriter. Using that same interface to enter data into a computer was more comfortable for the user. A synthesizer is not a MIDI controller, but it could be. A drum machine is not a MIDI controller, but it could be. Are you confused yet? Well, fasten your seatbelt!

Sampling

Consider the terms *sampling*, *loops*, *sample*, *sampler*, and *sequencer*. Many people get confused with these terms, and it's easy to understand why. *Sampling* is a compositional or performance technique that grew out of the hip-hop movement in the 1970s. Early hip-hop artists, such as Grandmaster Flash and DJ Cool Herc, would use records and turntables—like those used in radio stations—to transition between two records, combining the music from different songs. They would then rap their lyrics on top of the music to create a new original song. From this tradition came the practice of taking a section, or sample, of another song and using it to create a new song. These samples were typically short drum patterns or melodic phrases. This practice is called sampling. These short musical phrases were repeated over and over or looped. These samples came to be known as *loops*. Using pre-existing loops as the basis for a new song resulted in the compositional process known as sampling.

A *sampler* is an electronic device that was developed in the late 1970s that could be used to create original loops. A *drum machine* is a type of sampler (Figure 2.1). The device stores single pieces of recorded sounds that can be activated by pressing a key or pad. Think about striking a snare drum one time and recording that sound. Then repeat the process with each drum and cymbal in the drum kit. Each of these single pieces of recorded sounds is called a *sample*. The sampler was the electronic instrument that could playback these sounds manually or could be programmed to play the sounds in a particular pattern. These patterns could be saved and then played back to create loops. You can also take a sample and alter the pitch just like pitches are organized on a piano keyboard (Figure 2.2). The samples can now be performed melodically on the sampler to create loops that could be used in sampling. Make sense?

Roland TR-808 - Drum Machine
Figure 2.1

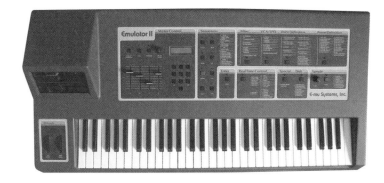

Emulator II - Sampling Synthesizer
Figure 2.2

These samplers became more sophisticated as the technology developed, allowing them to save multiple loops, combine the loops, or program a series of different loops to repeat a set number of times in whatever sequence the artist chose. Thus samplers evolved into *sequencers*, or devices that could be used to map out entire songs. As the number of new devices increased, the amount of equipment that had to be lugged around by performing DJs or crammed into recording studios became substantial (Figure 2.3).

Figure 2.3

Enter the Computer

Personal computers had been introduced to the consumer market by the late 1970s. By the early 1980s, consumers wanted to use these new electronic and digital music-making tools with the personal computer. This led to the development of the MIDI platform in 1983, which standardized the digital format for all manufacturers. Work was also beginning on the creation of a single platform that could combine synthesizers, sampling, looping, samples, samplers, sequencers, MIDI controllers, recording, audio editing, and mixing in the digital world. 1985 saw a company called Digidesign develop an audio editing software called Sound Designer. Sound Designer was developed into a compatible software package for Apple computers and was reintroduced in 1989 as Sound Tools (Figure 2.4a). The capabilities of Sound Tools were greatly expanded in the following two years, resulting in what would become the first industry-standard digital audio workstation, ProTools (Figure 2.4b).

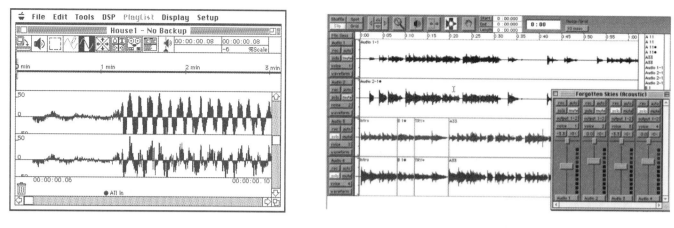

Digidesign Sound Tools
Figure 2.4a

Pro Tools 1.1
Figure 2.4b

Digital Audio Workstation

Other companies followed in developing other versions of a DAW. Examples include Logic Pro, Reaper, Cubase, Ableton Live, Reason, FL Studio, Sonar, and Studio One. Soundtrap is a cloud-based DAW that began as a small start-up company from Sweden and was later bought out (and now owned) by Spotify. Soundtrap by Spotify has quickly become a viable option for home studio music producers and educational settings, particularly with podcasting.

What Is a DAW?

The simple definition is that a DAW is an app or software package used to record, edit, and produce audio files. The DAW created a way to bring acoustic, electric, analog audio, digital music, and production technologies together into a single platform on a single device.

A major omission of this definition is that a DAW is first and foremost an organizational tool. Music and songs have structure and organization called *form*. Without form, music would be a confusing or unfinished-sounding collection of snippets and random sounds. A digital tool that can be used to organize music into a formal structure is called a *sequencer*. A DAW is also a sequencer used to synchronize and organize sounds chronologically.

The organization first takes place vertically in *tracks*. Tracks create an individual space for each instrument in a production to be organized so they can be created, edited, and crafted to work together with the other parts. The image below shows the instrumentation for a typical rock band and the tracks for each instrument (Figure 2.5). The sounds contained in each of the tracks are organized separately from each other. If all of the instruments were recorded on the same track, there would be no way to turn down the drums without turning down all the rest of the instruments.

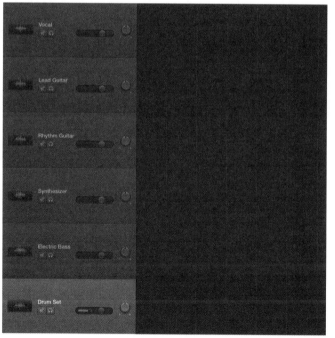

Figure 2.5

Sounds are added to the tracks in what are called *regions*. Regions are colored boxes that function as containers (Figure 2.6). All of the regions in this image contain audio, or real sound, made by real instruments. The image also shows how these sounds are organized in time. The drums start at the beginning, followed by the electric bass in the third bar. Then the synthesizer, rhythm guitars, and lead guitars enter at bar 5 before the vocal track enters at bar 9.

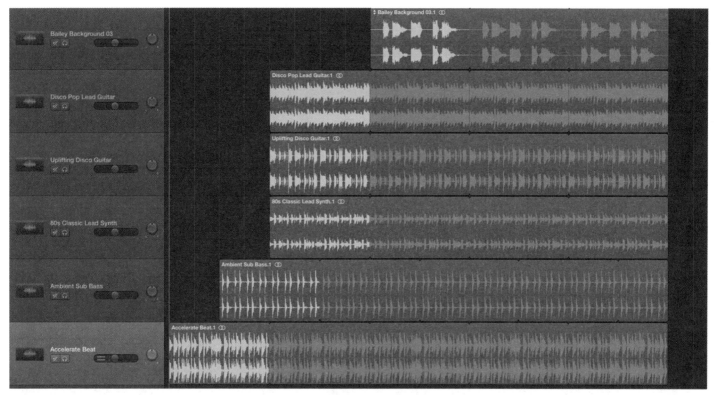

Figure 2.6

Recording

When you think about the word "record" in a musical context, it's natural to think about using a microphone or line input to record live audio into a recording device. You can record using this method in a DAW, which would result in regions like the ones shown in Fig. 2.6. Those regions contain recorded audio. But consider the general definition of the word "record." One definition of the verb form offered by Merriam-Webster states: "to register permanently by mechanical means." You could record a conversation by using an audio recording device, but you could also record the conversation with a written or typed transcript. A DAW can be used to record music similarly.

Music notation is a system of "writing down" music on a staff or score (Figure 2.7). Music notation software platforms have been developed so that music can be notated using a computer in much the same way that word processing software was developed to replace the pencil and pen or the typewriter. Examples include Finale, Noteflight, Sibelius, and Flat.io.

Figure 2.7

Traditional music notation is a means of recording music. Most music notation software is also capable of playing an audio version of the notated music. The software does this by converting the notated music into MIDI data. The DAW is capable of recording MIDI data directly without having to use traditional notation. This can be done using what is called *real-time entry* or *step entry* methods. The result is what I believe to be a new method of notating music: digital notation (Figure 2.8).

Figure 2.8

Notice in this image that the region for this track is a different color, and the information contained in the region looks much different than the squiggly lines of the audio track that was previously shown. This is because this region contains MIDI data rather than audio. MIDI data is a set of information that the computer will process to create virtual sounds. You can see how the computer digitally notates the music by taking a closer look at the MIDI track, sometimes referred to as a software track (Figure 2.9). The information notated (recorded) in the MIDI track shows, among other things, what pitch to play, when the pitch starts, and when it ends (duration). The *velocity* or loudness of the note is also recorded. This is essentially the same information that is communicated in traditional music notation: pitch, rhythm, and dynamics. I have spent much time debating with my classically trained music friends about the necessity of teaching traditional music notation. My opinion is that learning traditional music notation is not necessary in the context of the music technology lab/home studio.

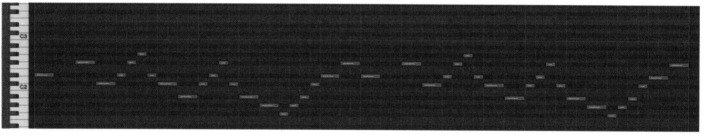

Figure 2.9

Editing ▶️

The DAW also allows the musician to edit the music that is recorded into the regions and tracks of the DAW. There is often some confusion in regards to what the difference is between music editing and music production. Some of the confusion is due to the lack of concise and clear consensus on the definitions. While there are certainly some nuanced distinctions and exceptions, the simplest definition I can offer is as follows:

- Editing is what the DAW enables you to do to craft individual tracks.
- Production is what the DAW enables you to do to craft all of the tracks together into a final product.

The editing functions in the DAW are similar to the editing processes in a word processor. A word processor allows you to cut, copy, and paste text in the document. You can identify and correct mistakes, add emphasis to certain words or phrases by adding **boldface**, *italics*, or underlining the text, change the color of the text, add highlights, or change the font, etc. There are parallels to each of these editing functions in a word processor with the editing capabilities of a DAW.

Music is very repetitive. This repetition creates patterns in the sounds and phrases of the music. The simplest way to create repetition is to copy and paste. A DAW allows the music producer to easily copy and paste regions in the DAW. You can also easily move regions with a click, drag, and drop using the mouse (Figure 2.10). By holding the OPTION or ALT button on the keyboard and then clicking, dragging, and dropping a region, you can copy and paste the region (Figure 2.11). Do you want to get rid of a region? Click on it to select it, then press DELETE on your keyboard (Figure 2.12). Voila! Gone!

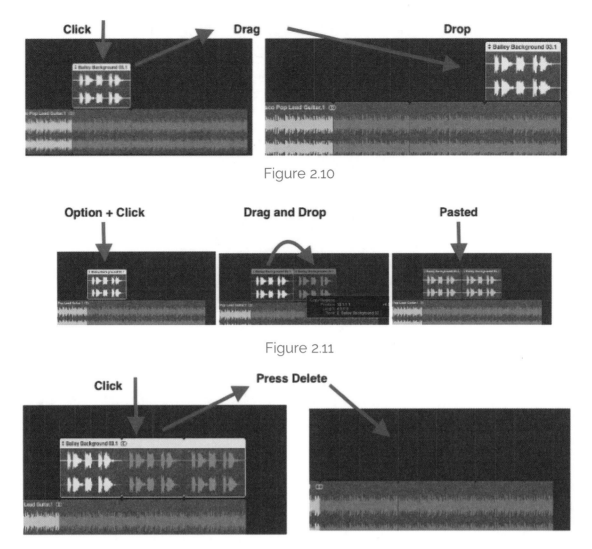

Figure 2.10

Figure 2.11

Figure 2.12

You can also use the same technique to correct individual pitches or rhythms in software (MIDI) tracks. Click on a pitch and drag it up or down to change the pitch (Figure 2.13). Or drag it side to side to change the rhythm (Figure 2.14). The OPTION + click, drag, and drop method works the same way to copy and paste individual pitches or groups of pitches. Click to select a region and then hit the DELETE button to delete. Easy!

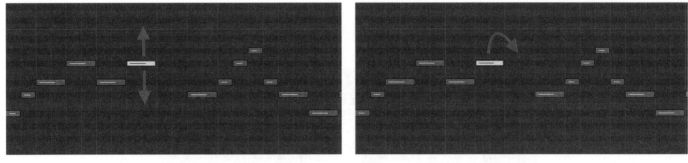

Figure 2.13   Figure 2.14

The DAW also provides a huge range of options for what are called *plug-in effects*. Since the early days of studio recording, music producers have searched for ways to alter or enhance the sounds of their recordings. Electronic devices were invented that would alter the sounds in a variety of ways. These electronic devices were mounted and stored in racks (Figure 2.15). The sounds were altered by running the sound output from a microphone or electric guitar with a cable and plugging it into one of these devices. Another cable would then run out of the device and be plugged into a mixer for playback. These devices were often used in combination by connecting them to each other with these cables and became known as plug-in effects. These same types of electronic devices are commonly used by electric guitar players also. The devices are usually mounted onto a piece of wood with the performer changing effects using their foot to press the buttons or pedals. These devices are known as *pedalboards* or footboards (Figure 2.16). The result from all of these plug-in devices often resembled a plate of spaghetti (Figure 2.17).

Figure 2.15

Figure 2.16

Figure 2.17

Many DAWs organized and simplified the use of plug-in effects by creating digital simulations of these effects that can be easily accessed and applied with a few clicks of the mouse (Figure 2.18). Reason Studios designed the interface for the digital version of plug-in effects with their DAW to look and feel like the physical version of plug-in effects (Figure 2.19). The Reason DAW may look very familiar and comfortable for someone with experience working in the analog world of music production but very intimidating for someone without that experience.

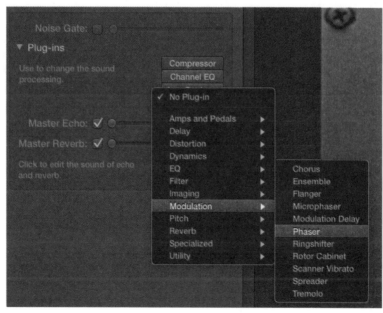

Figure 2.18

Figure 2.19

While there are many similarities in the capabilities and functions of available DAWs, the design of the interface is going to create workflows that will appeal to different users in different ways. It is important to take the time to research and explore the different applications available before deciding which DAW will best suit the needs of you and your students.

As mentioned earlier, some DAWs are only compatible with certain operating systems. Mixcraft, Cakewalk, Music Maker+ are PC only, whereas GarageBand and Logic Pro X are Apple/Mac only. Others are cross-platform, such as Pro Tools, Ableton Live, and Reaper. Soundtrap by Spotify offers a unique cloud-based platform that allows for remote collaboration and integrates with many learning management systems used by schools and universities. The intended use and skill level of the user is another important consideration. While GarageBand, Soundtrap, and FL Studio may be great options for novice music producers, they would feel very limited in capability to experienced users. Pro Tools, Ableton Live, and Reason have outstanding production capabilities but would likely feel overwhelming to the novice. Finally, price is another factor, with costs ranging from free to hundreds of dollars.

CHAPTER 3: CREATING, RECORDING, AND CAPTURING SOUNDS

Now that you have your lab or studio set up and an understanding of the tools that you have to work with, it's time to start making music! There are two methods of recording musical ideas into a DAW. One is step entry method, and the other is real-time entry. Keep in mind that when the term "record" is used, it's referring to the broad definition: to register permanently by mechanical means.

DAW Layout

The diagram below is of the Soundtrap DAW (Figure 3.1). The layout and elements of different DAWs will vary, but most will share the common elements labeled here. The *workspace* will be the large empty area where regions will be created, recorded, edited, and sequenced for the project. The *timeline* is the ruler that runs along the top edge of the workspace and is used to synchronize and align the regions that will be placed on the tracks. The *playhead* is a vertical line that moves along the timeline and can be used to align regions or indicate where regions will be placed on the timeline. It's analogous to a cursor in a word processing document. (In fact, sometimes it's called the *play cursor* in a DAW.) The column on the left side of the window, sometimes called the *track panel*, is where the *track headers* are located as different tracks are added to a project. The right side of the window is where most *loop libraries* will be found. Loops can often be filtered in several ways—by instrument, style, tempo, etc. There are other editing and production tools available that will be explored later.

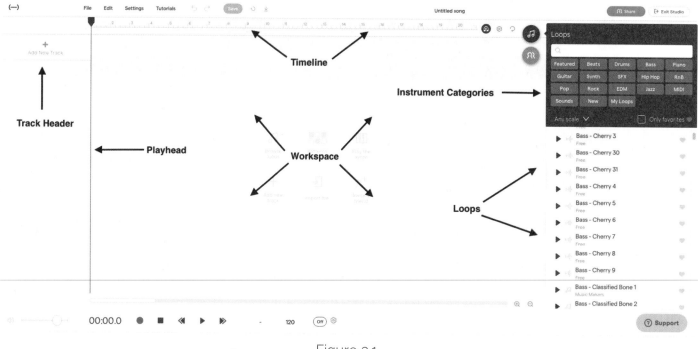

Figure 3.1

Step Entry Method

Step entry method is the process of placing digital audio or data into a track using a series of steps. This would be analogous to notating music onto a staff using manuscript paper and pencil or notation software. You are writing out the series of musical events (pitch, rhythm, duration, dynamics, etc.) that will only be heard once the notation is performed or played back.

The step entry method in a DAW is most often used to notate into a software track. Any process that requires using the mouse or trackpad to click-drag and drop regions in the DAW would be considered a step entry method. Therefore, copying and pasting a region or even moving a region would be considered step entry.

One of the quickest ways to create music in a DAW is by using the loop library. Most DAWs include a library of loops as part of the software package. Additional loop packs can be purchased from either the software developer or third-party providers and added to the loop library. Most loop libraries that come included in today's DAW software packages provide an ample amount of loops for the beginning or novice digital musician.

The simplest step entry technique would be selecting a loop to use, then dragging it onto the workspace. Notice that some loops are *audio loops*, while others are *software loops*. Audio and software loops must be placed on separate tracks. Audio and software tracks can be placed on top of each other and played simultaneously, but a track can only contain either audio regions or software regions (Figure 3.2).

Figure 3.2

Step entry method is also used to digitally notate or record musical ideas into the DAW. To do this, it's important to understand how digital music notation works. Anyone who has ever spent any time in an elementary or middle school music classroom has probably seen a large poster of the "Rhythm Tree" (Figure 3.3). This diagram shows the rhythmic relationships between the various rhythms that can be used to create music. These notation symbols are then organized linearly on a music score to indicate when the pitch will sound within the measure and how long the sound will last (Figure 3.4).

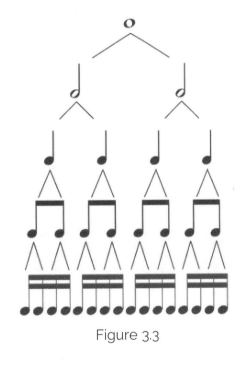

Figure 3.3

Figure 3.4

Digital rhythm works in the same way but uses a different visual system. Notice that the timeline along the top edge of the workspace in Fig. 3.1 looks like a ruler. This ruler doesn't measure physical length or distance; it measures time and duration. In the same way that traditional rhythmic notation indicates when a sound will happen in time and how long that sound will last on a music staff, digital rhythmic notation accomplishes this on the timeline (Figure 3.5).

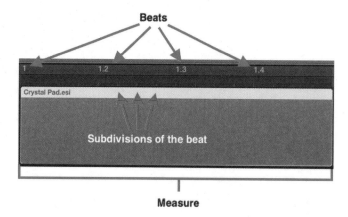

Figure 3.5

The digitally notated rhythm tree can then be expressed as illustrated below (Figure 3.6).

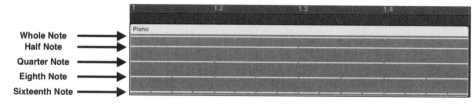

Figure 3.6

Traditional music notation also communicates which pitch should be sounded with the rhythmic patterns through the use of the lines, spaces, and ledger lines above and below the *staff*. Digital notation also communicates this information by switching to the "piano roll" view of the region. A piano keyboard is placed vertically on the left edge of this view, aligned with a grid, where specific pitches can be placed with the desired rhythmic pattern (Figure 3.7).

Figure 3.7

The benefit of using the step entry method to record music is that it's very accurate and precise. The drawback is that it can be a slow and tedious process, and that brings us to the second option: *real-time entry*.

Real-Time Entry Method

The *real-time entry* method is exactly what it says it is: entering the musical data into the software track as it happens in real time. It essentially feels like recording a live music performance, and it is. The only difference is that, instead of recording audio, you're recording MIDI data into the track. It's like typing words into a word processor simultaneously as you are speaking. Easier said than done, literally!

This is where the real power of MIDI controllers can be utilized. The QWERTY keyboard connected to your computer is a MIDI controller. You can use that keyboard to enter note data into the track (Figure 1.5), but if the creator is comfortable playing the piano, drums, saxophone, or guitar, there are MIDI instruments to facilitate entering the data in real time using a device that feels musically natural. Examples of these MIDI controllers are pictured at the end of Chapter 1. MIDI controllers are usually "plug and play" (no driver download or interface required) and connect directly to a desktop or laptop computer using a USB cable. The MIDI controller may feel like a piano or drum set to the creator, but as far as the computer is concerned, it may as well be the QWERTY keyboard. The device is not sending any actual sound or audio to the DAW—only data. Once the data is in the software track, the DAW can change the sound to be any instrument chosen in the sample library (Figure 3.8).

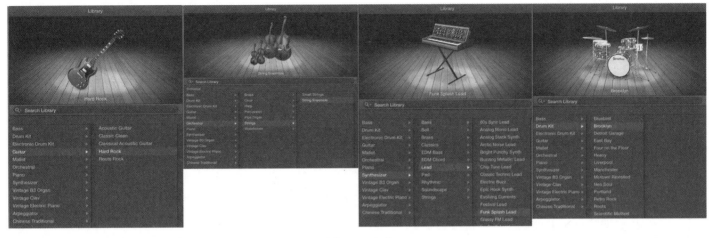

Figure 3.8

Real time feels and looks like recording audio with a recording device. The first step is to create a track in the DAW and make sure that you have that track selected. Set the tempo to the desired speed and make use of the built-in metronome or click track to help you enter the data as accurately as possible. Place the playhead where you want the DAW to begin recording and click on the record button in the transport controls. Wait for the count-off, and then perform the part on the MIDI controller (Figure 3.9).

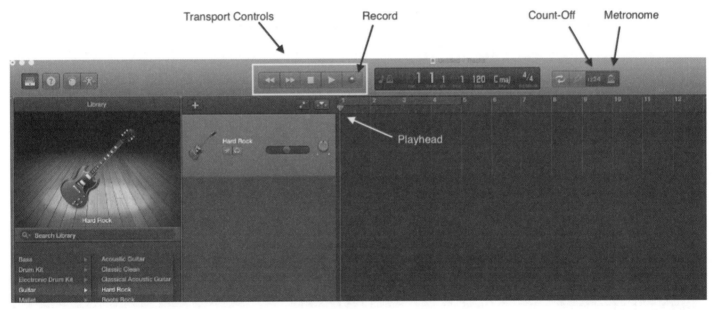

Figure 3.9

Look closely at the example below and you will notice that there are several places where the notes that were recorded do not quite line up with the grid of the timeline (Figure 3.10). This is because the computer captures the exact moment that a key was played, down to the millisecond, and it is very difficult for even professional musicians to perform with absolute rhythmic accuracy.

Figure 3.10

This illustrates the pros and cons of using real-time entry methods. A lot of data can be entered very quickly using real-time entry, but it can be imprecise. No worries though, as the DAW can easily fix these small rhythmic imperfections—should you choose to do so—using a function called *quantization*. When a software region is quantized, the computer takes the data points that were entered into the region and automatically shifts them to the nearest grid line according to the tolerance set by the user. This means the user can select if the DAW should adjust the data to the nearest beat, half beat, quarter beat, etc. (Figure 3.11).

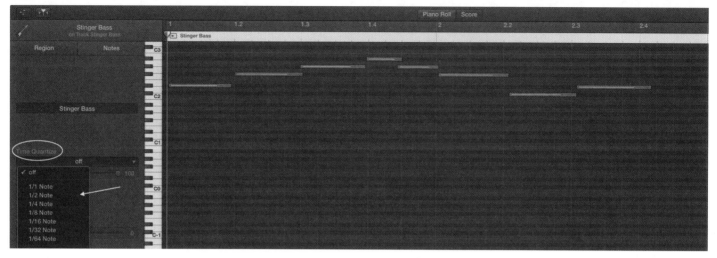

Figure 3.11

Notice the difference after quantization is applied to the example (Figure 3.12).

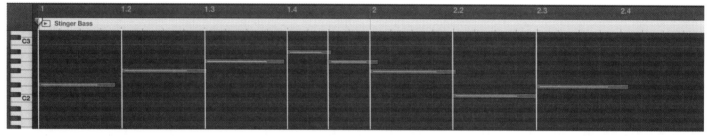

Figure 3.12

The beginning of each note is now aligned with the timeline grid, but notice that the length of the notes is not aligned or consistent. Most DAWs will not quantize the duration of the notes by default—only where the note begins. Many will allow you to quantize note length as well by adjusting the quantization parameters. If your DAW doesn't allow this, you can use step entry methods to make final adjustments to the duration of each pitch by using the mouse to click and drag the end of the note to the desired duration (Figure 3.13).

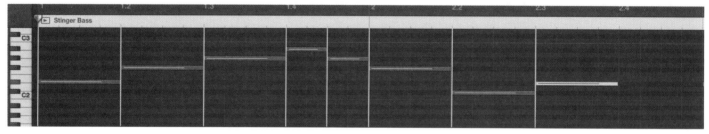

Figure 3.13

Quantization can also be used with audio regions, though the process for the DAW is a bit different than quantizing software regions. Recording audio requires the use of an interface to translate audio signals into digital data for the computer. This interface is integrated into USB microphones. The use of an electronic XLR microphone or line input from an electric guitar or synthesizer, however, will require a peripheral audio interface between the source and the computer (Figure 1.7). Recording audio into the DAW results in a region that contains a *waveform* (Figure 3.14). This waveform is a visual representation of sound expressed in *amplitude* (volume) and *frequency* (pitch) over time.

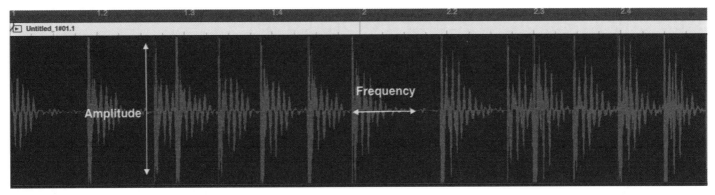

Figure 3.14

The DAW identifies *transients* in the waveform. A transient is a high-amplitude, short sound at the beginning of a waveform. Musicians would refer to this as the "attack" at the beginning of the note. If you traced the outline of the amplitude for the waveform in the previous example, it looks like a series of triangles (Figure 3.15).

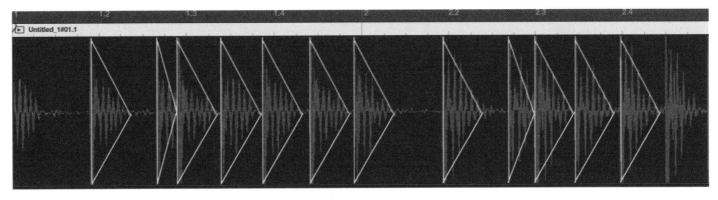

Figure 3.15

The transient would be the highest level of the amplitude measured vertically in the sound. Notice in the example how the transients do not line up with the marks on the timeline ruler (Figure 3.16).

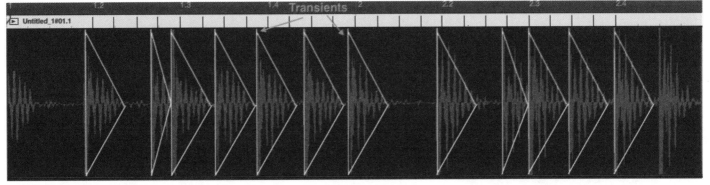

Figure 3.16

When quantizing audio regions, the DAW identifies the transients and uses a process known as "time-flex" to compress or extend the waveform to align the transients with the timeline. Note that the compression of one waveform results in the extension of another and vice versa (Figure 3.17).

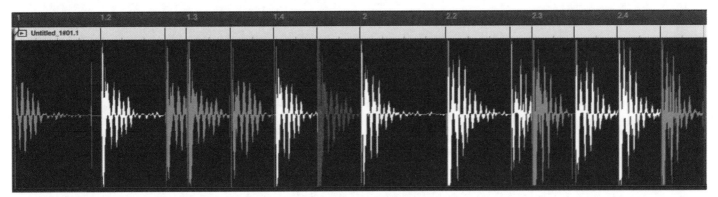

Figure 3.17

Step Entry Lesson: Creating a Drum Loop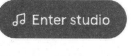

This lesson will use the Soundtrap DAW to create a drum loop using the Patterns Beatmaker tool in the DAW.

1. Enter the Studio in Soundtrap to start a new project.

   ♫ Enter studio

2. Select a *Music project*.

   Music

3. Then select *Patterns Beatmaker* in the center of the workspace.

   Browse loops   Patterns BeatMaker   Play the synth

   Add new track   Import file   Invite a friend

4. This will open a window at the bottom half of the screen with a 4x3 grid of boxes that represent the instruments of the drum set and four beats subdivided into 16th-note blocks.

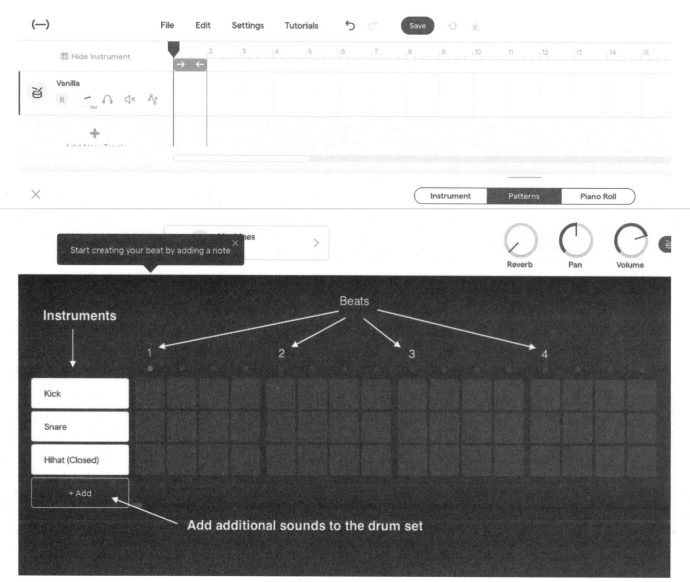

5. Add sounds to create your drum pattern by clicking on a box in the grid. The example below illustrates a basic drum pattern with the kick drum on beats 1 and 3, the snare drum on beats 2 and 4, and a hi-hat cymbal playing eighth notes across the measure.

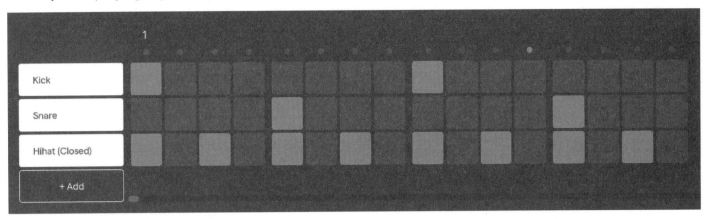

6. To create the loop, copy the first measure into measures 2, 3, and 4. You can do this by holding down OPTION/ALT and click-dragging and dropping the region into the next measure.

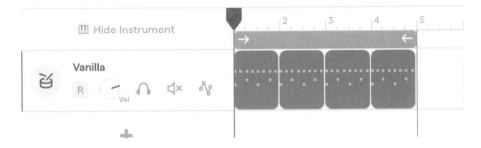

7. Rather than repeat one measure over and over, create a "turnaround" (or "fill") in the fourth measure. The turnaround breaks up the strict repetition of the drum patterns and signals the end of one musical phrase. Turnarounds are typically added at the end of either four- or eight-measure phrases. To do this, double-click on the region in the fourth measure to bring the *Patterns Beatmaker* window back and move the playhead to the beginning of the fourth measure. I added three instruments to the grid: high tom, mid tom, and low tom. Finally, I deleted the kick, snare, and hi-hat notes on beats 3 and 4 and added notes for the high, mid, and low tom to break up the repetition and end the phrase.

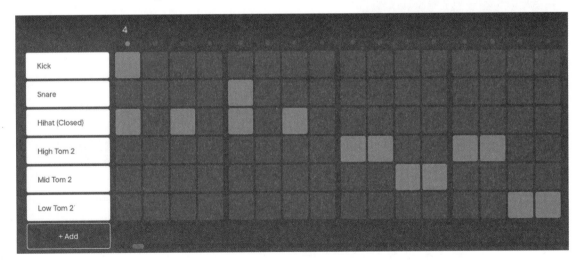

8. Listen to the result.

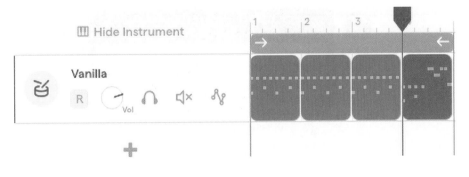

9. To create a loop that can be added to the loop library, you must first merge the four regions into a single region. Select all four regions by clicking in an area below the regions then dragging across all four regions while holding down the mouse button. When you release the mouse, all regions should be highlighted. Then click on *Edit* in the drop-down menu and select *Merge Regions*.

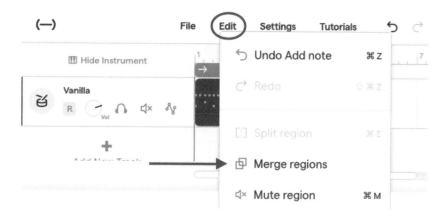

10. You should now see a single region for the four-measure phrase.

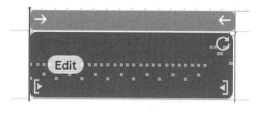

11. Hover the mouse in the region, and an *Edit* button will appear. Click on *Edit* and select *Add to loop library*.

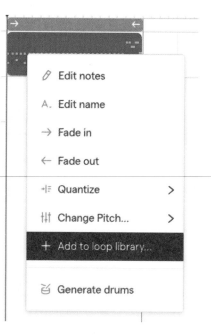

12. Give your loop a name and click *Save*. You have now added your own original loop to the loop library that can be used for any future projects.

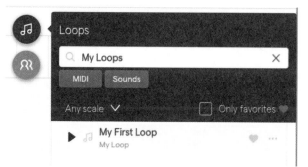

Real-Time Entry Lesson: Creating a Bass Loop

This lesson will use the GarageBand DAW and the Akai MPK Mini Keyboard MIDI controller to create a bass loop.

1. Create a new empty project in GarageBand.

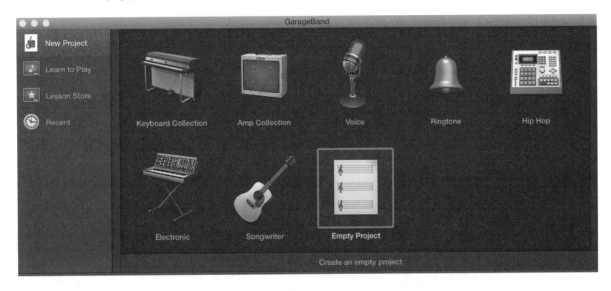

2. Use the instrument sample library to choose a bass sound that you want to use.

3. Add a drum loop from the loop library to play along with and enable the cycle bar by clicking on the cycle button. You can adjust the length of the cycled region by clicking on the end of the cycle bar and dragging to the desired length.

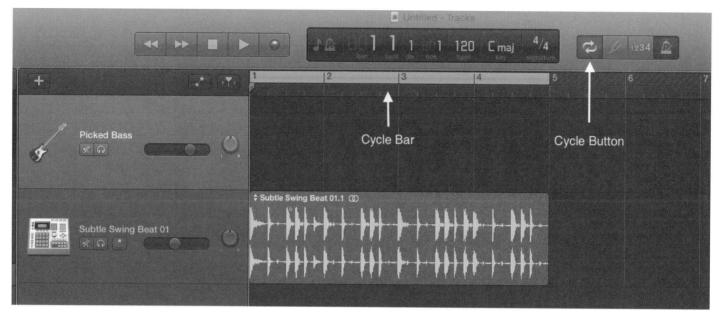

4. With the keyboard MIDI controller connected to the computer via USB cable, you should be able to play the bass guitar sounds in the bass track. The bass loop will be created using the E♭ minor pentatonic scale on the MIDI controller. This is a great scale to use for the novice musician because it utilizes only the black keys on the keyboard. Start by playing the second black key from the left end of the keyboard. This is the note E♭. Then play each black key in succession moving from left to right until reaching the second E♭ marked on the keyboard diagram. Once the high E♭ is reached, reverse the process and play each black key moving back to the left. When the low E♭ is reached again, play the D♭ below it and then return to the E♭. That is the E♭ minor pentatonic scale.

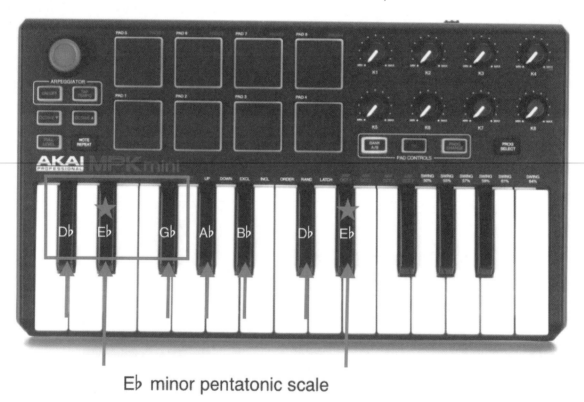

E♭ minor pentatonic scale

5. Now the fun part begins! With the cycle bar enabled, press play on the transport controls to hear the drum loop that was added earlier. Experiment and improvise a bass line starting with just the note E♭. Once you get a feel for the groove and develop some rhythmic ideas, add the notes D♭ and G♭ that are below and above the E♭. Continue to add other notes in the scale as you become more comfortable.

6. As you experiment and improvise, you should begin to focus on a rhythmic and melodic pattern to record into the DAW. There are several items to check to make sure the DAW is set correctly before you record: 1) Select the bass track by clicking on the track header; 2) Set the playhead at the beginning; 3) Turn the cycle bar off; 4) Enable the count-in button. When you are ready, click the record button on the transport controls.

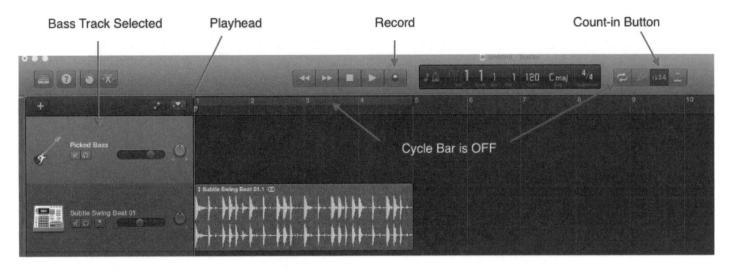

7. When you reach the end of the phrase, press the space bar to stop the recording. You should see a region appear with your bass loop data recorded into the region.

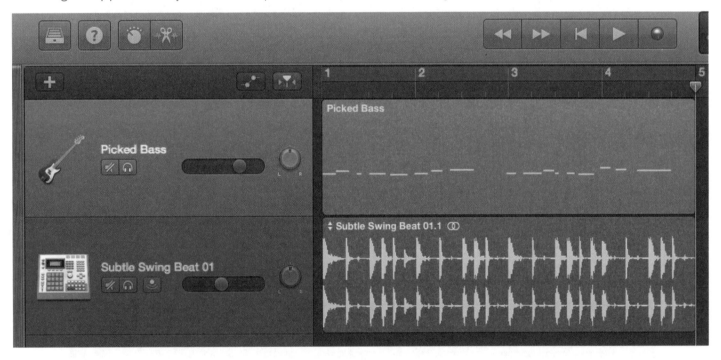

8. Now listen to what you have recorded along with the drum loop. You may notice that not all of the rhythms sound quite right with the drum loop. This is because you are human, and it is very difficult to perform with absolute rhythmic accuracy and precision. Double-clicking on the region will open the *editor window* where you can see these rhythmic errors more easily.

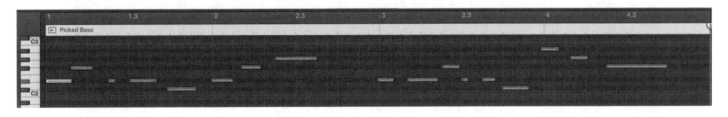

These errors can be fixed with a few clicks of the mouse to apply quantization to the region. Listen to the result and make any necessary changes.

A few more clicks will clean up the note lengths, and you have a bass loop ready to add to the loop library.

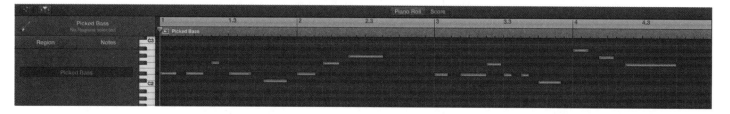

9. Give your bass loop a name by right-clicking on the region. Then click on *File* in the drop-down menu at the top of the screen and select *Add Region to Loop Library*.

Fill in a few pieces of information, and you have added your first bass loop to the loop library.

CHAPTER 4: FORM

Imagine that someone gave you a huge pile of wood, bricks, saws, hammers, and nails and asked you to build a house. You know what houses look like. There should be walls, doors, windows, a roof, rooms inside, maybe a garage, but where would you start? How do all of those materials fit together? Having a blueprint, or a set of instructions to follow, would make building the house more manageable.

On a more realistic scale, what if you were asked to bake a cake? You know that a cake requires flour, sugar, eggs, milk, and the ingredients have to be mixed, placed in a baking pan, and baked in the oven. But how much flour, sugar, and milk do you need? What temperature should the oven be? How long should it bake? The easiest way to bake a cake would be to go to the grocery store and buy a box of cake mix. The key ingredients would be in the box, and instructions for additional ingredients would be on the back of the box.

A DAW is like a musical box of cake mix. It contains all of the ingredients that you need to create songs and compositions, but there are no directions on the back of the box to guide you through the process. This chapter will provide you with a process for creating blueprints or recipes for creating music.

Repetition
Music is very repetitive, and this repetition creates patterns. Do you remember these types of exercises when you were in elementary school?

What Comes Next?

These exercises are important for children to learn how to recognize visual patterns. We find repetition and patterns all around us: art, architecture, the clothes that we wear, the games that we play, etc. Patterns provide a way for us to organize and make sense of the world around us.

Music is also full of repetition and patterns. Recognizing and understanding those aural patterns provides a blueprint, recipe, or form(ula) for creating music. Musical *form* gives the songs that are created structure and shape. Without it, music would be random noise with no discernible beginning, middle, or end. Have you ever listened to someone talk on and on about nothing? It may be interesting for a time, but eventually you lose interest. That would be music without form.

Song Form
In the same way that there are many variations in recipes for baking cakes or blueprints for building houses, there are many variations in how a song can be structured. It is important to learn and become comfortable with basic forms before experimenting with variation and ornamentation.

A great example of a song form used in popular music is Taylor Swift's "Shake It Off" (Swift, Martin, Shellback, 2014). The song begins with her giving examples of things that people say about her that are not true. "They say I'm not very smart, I date around too much, but they always leave me." That's followed by her response to the gossip. "I can't change what other people think or do, so I don't let it bother me." Then she gives some examples of things that *are* true about her that people don't recognize. "I'm a very smart and unique person." That's once again followed by her response.

This is what is called *verse* and *chorus*. The verse of the song describes an action, provides examples, or provides a chronology of events. The chorus of the song provides a summary, moral, or message in response to the verse. As you think about the lyrics of your favorite song, notice that the lyrics of the verse change even though the music stays the same. The lyrics of the chorus are always repeated and accompanied by the same music, which is usually different from the music of the verse. The verse section is labeled as "A," and the chorus section is labeled as "B" when diagramming song form. "Shake It Off," like many other songs in popular music, would be diagrammed **A-B-A-B**.

It is easy to see the repetition and patterns of the song so far. Humans like repetition and pattern, but too much repetition can get uninteresting. Many songwriters will add a unique section to break up the repetition of the song. This section usually has music and lyrics that are completely different from the rest of the song. This section is referred to as the *break* or *bridge*. The bridge in "Shake It Off" is the section where Taylor raps about a specific encounter that she had with a former boyfriend and his new girlfriend. Switching to rapping is stylistically different than any other part of the song. This is followed by the message of the song that she most wants people to remember. When life gets you down and people treat you unfairly, don't let it bother you. Reject the criticism like the old cliché: water on a duck's back.

The basic form of the song would be diagrammed as **A-B-A-B-C-B-B**, but Taylor uses a common variation of this form by adding a *pre-chorus* before the first two choruses. So, the actual form could be diagrammed **A-(b)-B-A-(b)-B-C-B-B**. Notice that the song has nine sections, but only four of those sections are unique. The other five sections are repetitions of an existing section. A closer listen reveals that each section is a total of 16 measures made up of a two-part, eight-measure phrase that is repeated. Each section could be diagrammed as **a-b-a-b**. Therefore, each 16-measure section consists of only eight measures of unique music. Now let's do some math.

Nine sections in the song multiplied by 16 measures in each section: 9 x 16 = 144 measures in the song. There are only four unique sections, and each section only contains eight measures of unique music: 4 x 8 = 32. The other 112 measures are those 32 measures copied and pasted! This should make the task of creating a song much less intimidating for the novice songwriter. Give it a try!

A-B-A-B-C-B-B Lesson ▶️

The Soundtrap DAW will be used for this lesson, but the same procedure can be used with any DAW.

1. Open a new music project in the Soundtrap Studio.

2. Take the drum loop that was created in the Step Entry Lesson from Chapter 3 and add it to a track. You can repeat the four-measure loop by floating the cursor in the upper right-hand corner of the region. Then click and drag to measure 9.

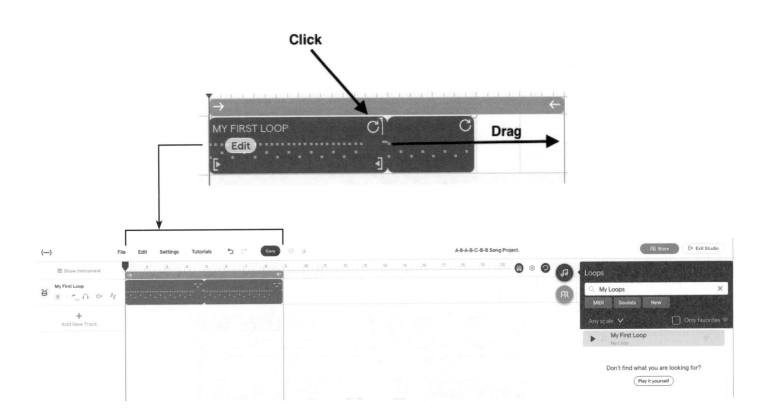

3. You can also use the bass loop created in Chapter 3 to add with the drum track.

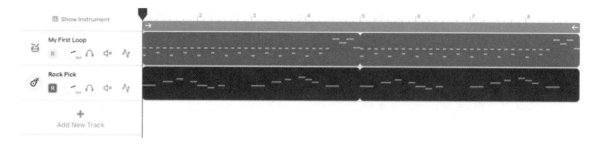

4. Next, add a guitar and keyboard track using loops from the loop library or create your own using step entry method or real-time entry with a MIDI instrument.

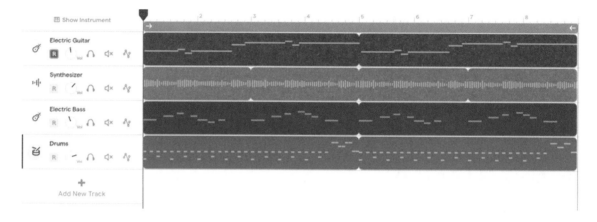

5. To complete the first A section of the song, just copy and paste the regions to repeat the phrase. Start by holding the COMMAND key (Apple) or the WINDOWS key (PC) and typing the letter "a." This should select and highlight all of the regions in the workspace. Next, hold OPTION (Apple) or ALT (PC) down, click and hold any of the selected regions, drag the regions over to measure 9, and drop them.

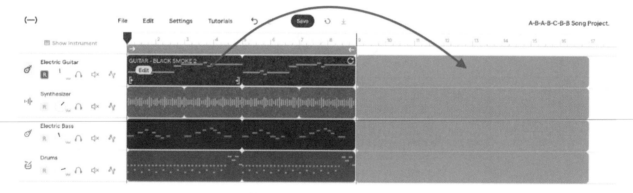

You now have your first A section completed.

6. Reposition the cycle bar to cycle measures 17–20 by clicking and dragging it down the timeline to measure 17. Repositioning the cycle bar makes it easier to experiment with different combinations of loops or improvise your ideas using a MIDI controller. Add a new drum, synthesizer, guitar, and bass loop for measures 17–20. Then use the loop function by floating the cursor in the upper right corner of each region and extending the phrases to measure 24.

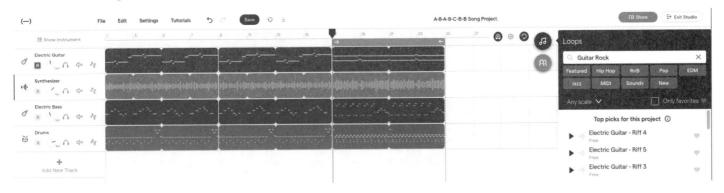

7. To complete the B section, copy and paste the eight-measure phrase again. Do not use the "Copy All" command since only the new four-measure phrase needs to be copied. To do this, start with the cursor just below the bottom track at the new phrase. Then click and drag across all four tracks to highlight the regions in the B sections. Now hold the OPTION/ALT key down and then click, drag, and drop the phrase at measure 25. At this point, you'll need to zoom out a bit to see everything that you've created thus far.

16 measure A section   16 measure B section

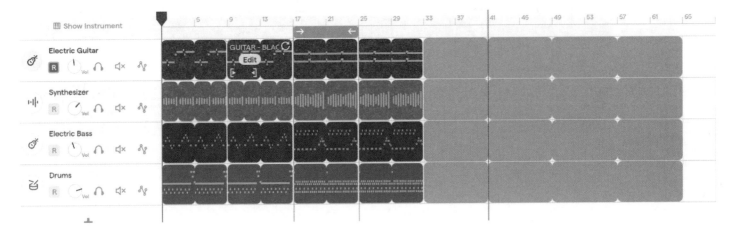

8. Now you've created the first A and B section of your song. The next step in the recipe for the song form is to repeat these sections. Use the zoom control to zoom out until you can see measures 1 to 65 on the timeline ruler. Use the *Select All* key command to select all of the regions in the workspace.

Hold down the OPTION/ALT key and click on any region to drag all of the selected regions and drop at measure 65.

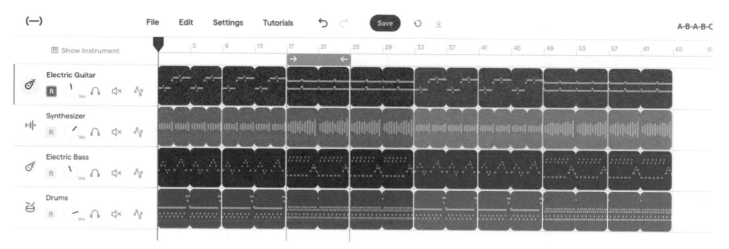

9. Reposition the cycle bar to measure 65–68. This will be the break (or bridge) for the song. This section is usually distinctly different from the A or B sections in style, key, or instrumentation. Create a four-measure phrase for the bridge using either the loop library or a MIDI controller. Then loop the four-measure phrase to repeat. The bridge is typically shorter than the A and B sections. It's only eight measures long in this example.

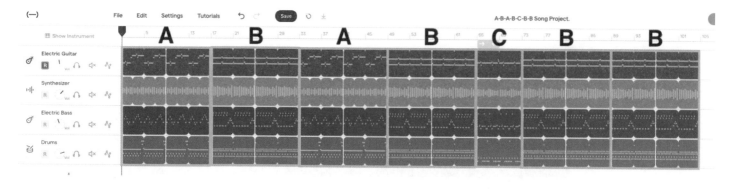

10. The last step to finish the form is to copy and paste the B section two times after the bridge. Use the scroll bar and zoom controls to position the workspace as needed. Use the OPTION + click, drag, and drop process to make copies of the B section.

11. The completed song should be 104 measures long. Now go back and give it a listen!

CHAPTER 5: HARMONY

Harmony is the element of music concerning chords and chord progressions. It's a foundational part of music and plays a key role in creating the aural environment of the song. Songs can be made to sound happy, bright, dark, moody, reflective, etc., through the creative and informed use of harmony. In da Vinci's famous painting the Mona Lisa, Lisa would be the melody, while harmony would be everything else around her—i.e., the background, texture, and colors surrounding her. The Mona Lisa would be a very different painting if there was a bright sun, beach, ocean waves, and a beach ball in her hand. Harmony can transform a song in a similar way.

Harmony is traditionally taught using manuscript paper to spell chords and chart out progressions, but that approach has little relevance to creating music in a home studio or music technology lab. What is important is understanding how scales are constructed on a piano keyboard, how chords are built on top of these scale notes, and, most importantly, what those chords sound like when played in a progression.

The diagram below illustrates the notes of a C major scale on a keyboard (Figure 5.1).

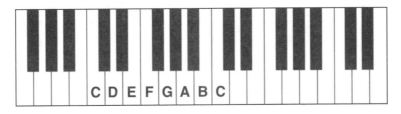

Figure 5.1

Instructions for playing these chords and progressions will refer to the fingers on your right hand as numbers 1–5 (Figure 5.2).

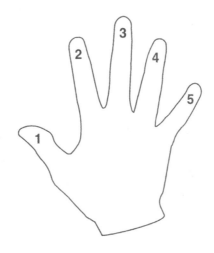

Figure 5.2

Play the notes C-E-G with fingers 1-3-5 of your right hand using a MIDI piano keyboard (Figure 5.3).

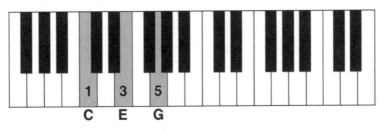

Figure 5.3

This chord would be named the "I" chord—i.e., "1" in Roman numerals—in the key of C, because the chord is built with the 3rd and 5th notes above the note C (Figure 5.4).

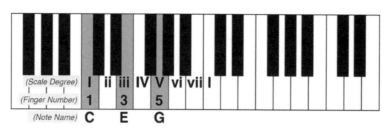

Figure 5.4

You could play each chord in the key of C by holding your right hand in this shape and shifting your hand to the right, one note each time (Figure 5.5).

 Chords in C Major

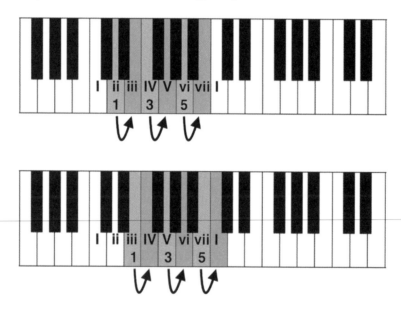

Figure 5.5

Continue this progression up and down the scale (Figure 5.6).

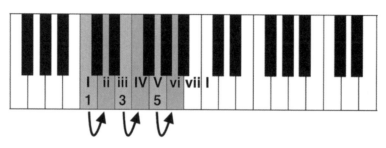

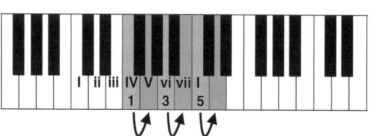

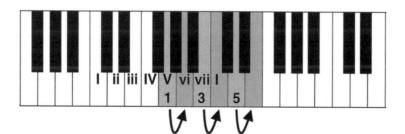

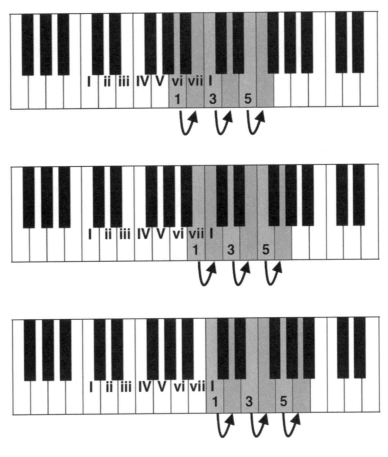

Figure 5.6

This is one way to identify and play all of the chords in the key of C. But chords are not typically played this way, and not all chords in a key are typically used in one musical phrase. A *chord progression* is a sequence of chords that's repeated over and over in a song as phrases are repeated. Remember: music is very repetitive!

One common chord progression in popular music is the I–V–vi–IV progression. The following sequence of four illustrations shows how this progression would be played on the keyboard by moving the fingers to the nearest notes of the next chord (Figure 5.7).

▶ I–V–vi–IV Progression

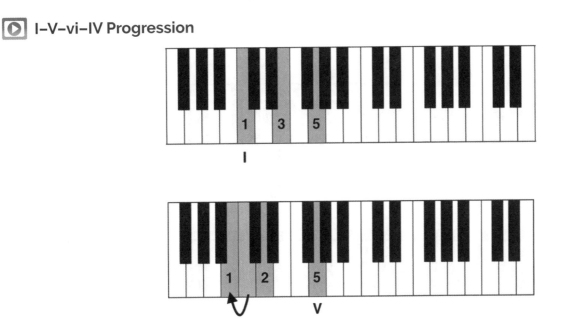

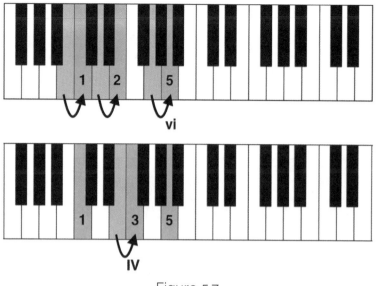

Figure 5.7

Practice playing this progression very slowly with your right hand. Gradually speed up the tempo of the chord changes as you get more comfortable playing the progression. Then try recording the progression into the DAW.

Chord progressions in minor keys provide a whole new palette of harmony to use in creating music. A common minor key chord progression in popular music is the i–III–VI–VII progression. This one is a little trickier but can be mastered with a little practice and persistence. This example below is in the key of A minor (Figure 5.8).

▶ i–III–VI–VII Progression

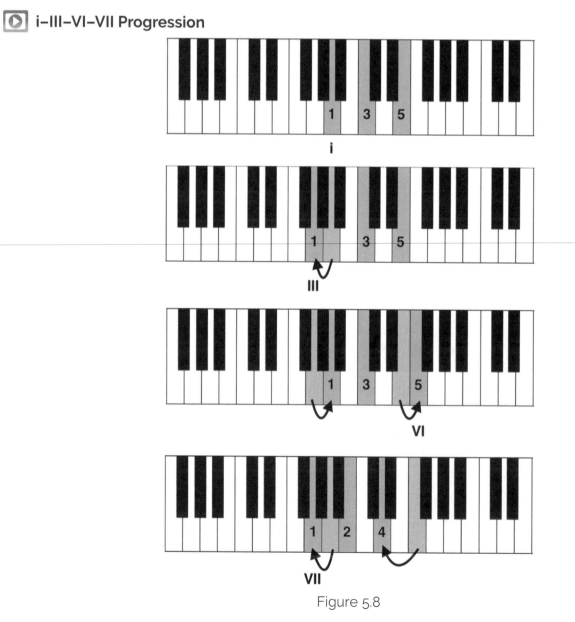

Figure 5.8

Work on playing this four-chord progression very slowly. Remember to only move the fingers that have to move. Notice in the illustrated i–III–VI–VII progression that the third finger stays in place for the i, III, and VI chords. It only moves to play the note B in the VII chord. Practice keeping it on the note C until it needs to move to B in the last chord.

One of the great things about these two progressions (there are others) is that the chords in the progression can be arranged in a different sequence to create some harmonic variety between the sections of your song. Take the I–V–vi–IV progression and try swapping the V and IV chords in the progression: I–IV–vi–V.

▶ **Chord Progression Variations**

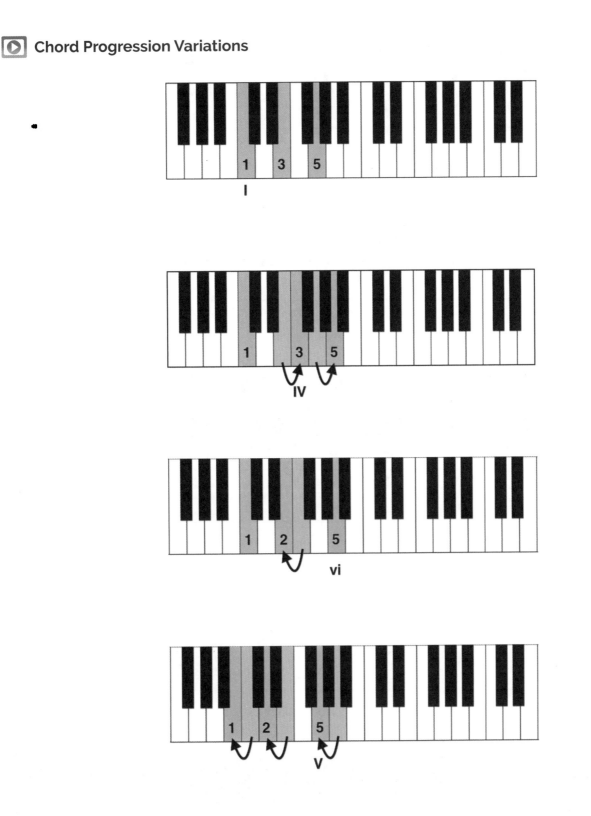

Figure 5.9

Or try this variation of the A minor progression: i–VII–III–VI.

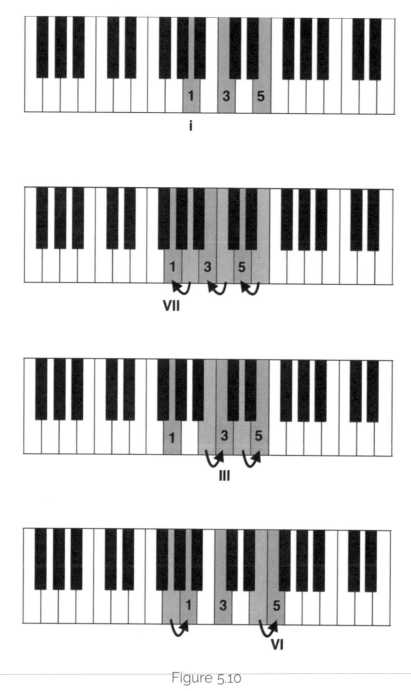

Figure 5.10

Step Entry Harmony Lesson ▶

This lesson will take you through the steps to create two different chord progressions using the step entry method.

1. Begin by opening a new project in your DAW. We'll use GarageBand for this lesson.

2. Create a software track. Then create a region by holding down the COMMAND/WINDOWS button and clicking in measure 1 of the track. When the region appears, float the cursor near the bottom-right edge of the region. You should see the cursor transform into double arrows. Click and drag to the right until the region extends through measure 4.

3. Double-click on the region to open the editor window on the bottom half of the screen.

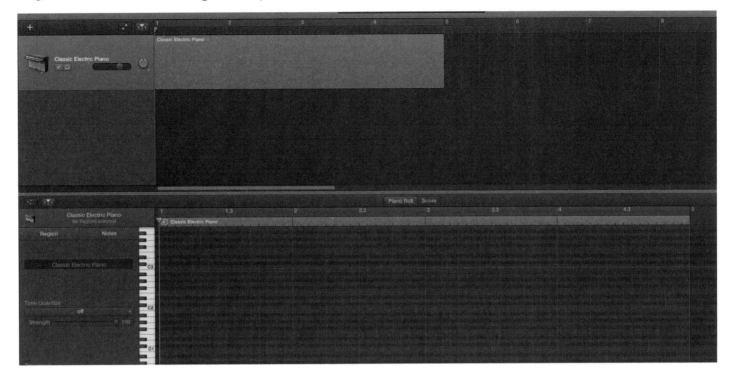

4. Use the diagram in Fig. 5.8 to enter the notes on the piano roll in the editor window. The notes of the first chord in Fig. 5.8 are A-C-E. Use the keyboard diagram on the left edge of the editor screen to locate the note A. Hold down the COMMAND/WINDOWS (C/W) button and you should see the cursor transform into a pencil. This is called the *pencil tool*. While holding down the C/W button, click on the row extending from the A note on the piano diagram. You should see a bar appear for the note A (Figure 5.11). Extend the length of the note to the end of the measure by clicking on the right edge of the bar and dragging it to the end of the measure (Figure 5.12).

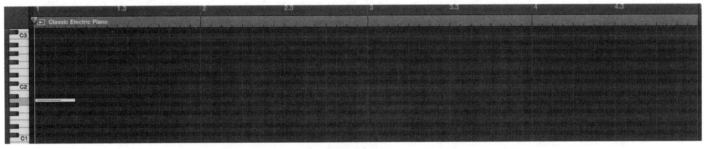

Figure 5.11

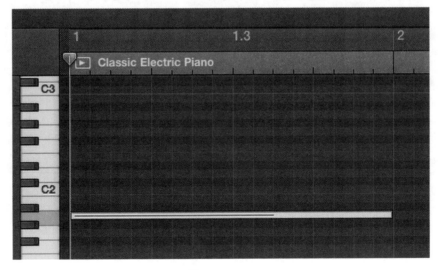

Figure 5.12

5. Use the same process to enter the notes C and E above the A. Once you set the note length for the A, it should enter the C and E for the same rhythmic value.

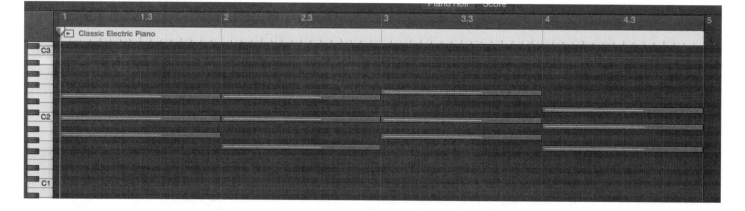

6. Repeat this process to enter the chords from Fig. 5.8. Each chord should take up one full measure.

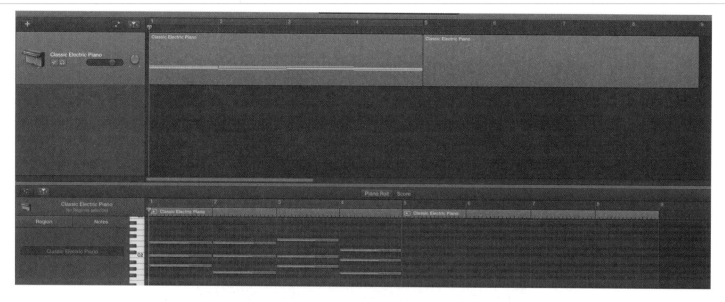

7. Now create another region for measures 5–8 by holding down the C/W button and clicking under measure 5 on the track in the workspace. Resize to extend the region through measure 8 and double-click to open the editor window.

8. Use Fig. 5.10 to enter the chord progression variation in measures 5–8. Listen to the result!

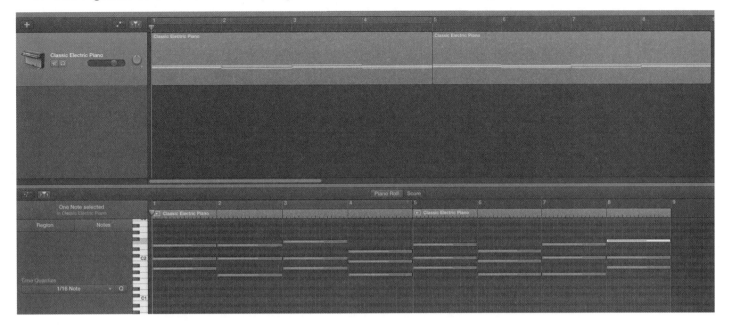

Real-Time Entry Harmony Lesson ▶

Step entry is a very precise method of entering MIDI data into the DAW, but it is time consuming. Being able to play a MIDI instrument and recording in real time can speed up the process dramatically. You will use the chord progressions illustrated in Figs. 5.7 and 5.9 for this lesson.

1. Now that you've spent some time practicing the C major chord progression, you're ready to record it into the DAW using real-time entry. Open a new project in your DAW with a software track. You won't need to create regions with this lesson. The DAW will automatically create the region when recording in real time. Make sure that you have the count-in and metronome turned on before you start recording.

2. Click on the red record button in the transport controls, wait for the count-off, and then play each chord for four counts—i.e., one chord per measure.

3. Press the space bar on the computer keyboard to stop the recording. You may notice that not all of the notes are aligned with the timeline grid.

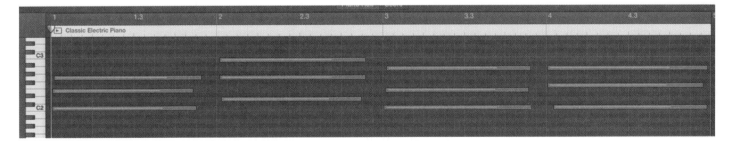

4. This can easily be corrected by using the *quantize* tool. Make sure that the region is selected on the track and in the editor window. Click on quantize and select "1/4 note" (Figure 5.13). You should see all of the notes in the region adjust to line up with beat 1 at the beginning of each measure.

Figure 5.13

You will have to adjust the length of each note manually using the mouse, but the beginning of each note should now be aligned with the timeline grid (Figure 5.14).

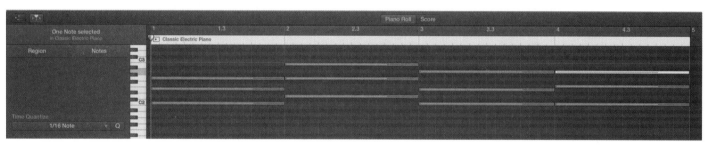

Figure 5.14

5. Now make sure that the playhead is placed at the beginning of measure 5. This is where the DAW will begin recording the variation of the chord progression. Click the record button again and record the second chord progression in measures 5–8. If you make a mistake, you can always delete the region, reset the playhead, and record again. When you're finished recording, quantize the region, adjust the note lengths as needed, and listen to your recording.

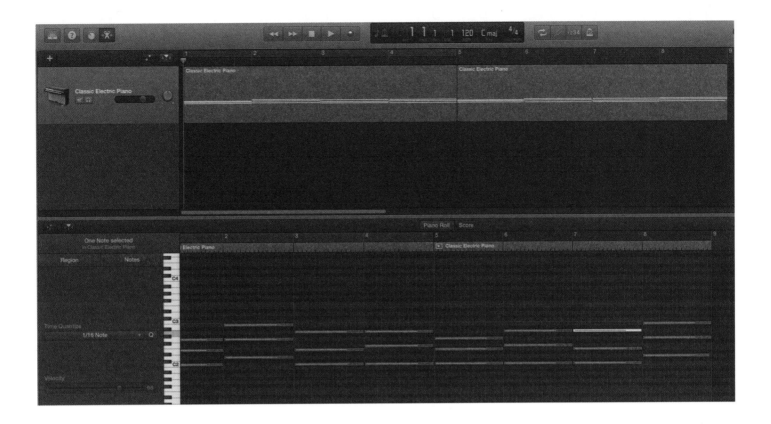

Creating Rhythmic Harmony

Many songs will need to have some rhythmic interest added to the harmony. This lesson demonstrates one way to create rhythmic harmony using the step entry method with the Soundtrap DAW.

1. Enter the Studio and click on *Play the Synth* in the middle of the workspace.

Browse loops

Patterns BeatMaker

Play the synth

Add new track

Import file

Invite a friend

2. Click on the *Piano Roll* button to view the piano roll grid.

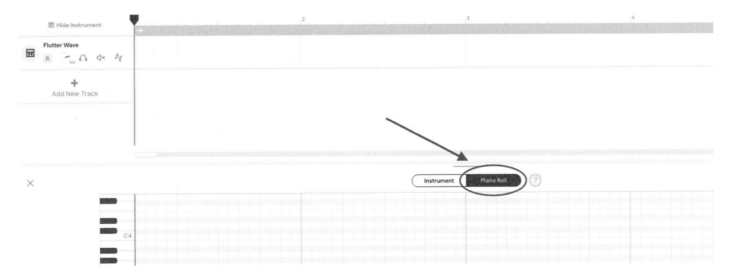

3. Click on the *Gear* button near the upper right corner of the window and set the timeline grid to 1/8 note.

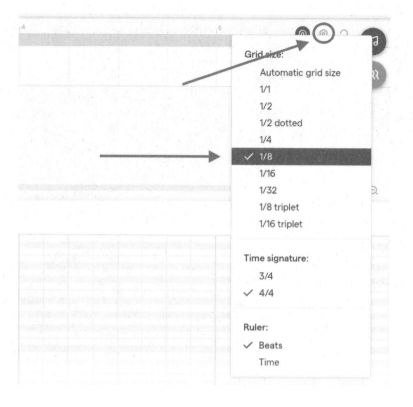

4. The Soundtrap DAW will allow the user to click on the pencil tool button so you do not have to hold down the C/W button while entering notes. Use the pencil tool to enter the notes of the C major chord in the first column of measure 1.

Pencil Tool

5. After you enter the notes for the C major chord, switch to the pointer tool, click and drag across the three notes to highlight, and use the OPTION + click, drag, and drop to copy and paste the notes into the next column.

2. Click and drag across to select

1. Switch to Pointer

C2, Velocity 100

3. Option + click, drag, and drop to copy and paste

6. Repeat this process until you have created eight columns of the chord.

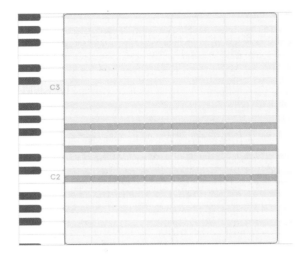

7. Extend the region to measure 5. Repeat the steps above for each of the chords from Fig. 5.7. Listen to the result when you finish. You should hear the chords pulsing out eighth notes. Note that this is not the most interesting rhythmic pattern.

8. Experiment with deleting a few columns of notes in the first measure to create a rhythmic pattern. Once you create a pattern that you like, apply the same pattern to the other measures by deleting columns. Listen to the result when you are finished. Much more interesting!

You could record a harmonic rhythmic pattern in real time using a MIDI controller, but if you are not comfortable doing that, this is an option to consider.

CHAPTER 6: MELODY

Melody is the element of music concerning the rhythmic sequence of pitches that are the primary focus of a song or composition. Different parts of a song can be melodic, but the melody is the part of the song that will get stuck in your head. If harmony is the background scene of the Mona Lisa, then melody is Lisa herself. Melody is what will be used to deliver the lyrics of a song, the string of notes flowing from the guitar solo at the bridge, or the tune that starts in your head before becoming your next musical creation.

A melody can be described in terms of its key, contour, duration, and style, but teaching someone how to write a great melody can be elusive. Exploration and experimentation are key. Developing a melody is ultimately a process of discovery.

Elements of Melody

The vast majority of music ever created, and virtually all of the music that is streamed and played on radio today, is *tonal*. Tonal means that the music is based on a scale. There are many different types of scales—major, minor, modal, pentatonic, etc.—but all of these scales are based around a central pitch called the *tonic note*. The tonic would be the first note of the scale. Some people have described writing melodies or harmonies as a process of establishing home, leaving home, sometimes getting lost, and then returning home again. This can be illustrated by playing a C major scale. Start on the note C and then play D, E, F, G, A, B, and stop. Stopping on the note B without continuing to C sounds very unfinished or incomplete. Go ahead and play the last note C. Feels good, right?

Range and Contour

Most trained vocalists have a usable range around two octaves (less for untrained vocalists). Most melodies don't use the full range of a vocalist, but it's important to know where the boundaries are. The example below illustrates a melody that covers the range of one octave from C4 to C5. The contour of the melody moves from low to high, peaking in the middle of the phrase before working its way back down at the end. The melody starts on the tonic note C and ends on the note where it started (Figure 6.1).

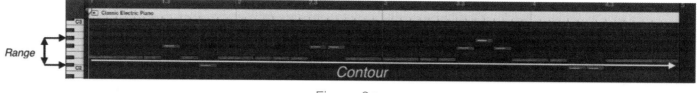

Figure 6.1

Melodies can also have a fairly flat contour and limited range with a lot of repetition (Figure 6.2).

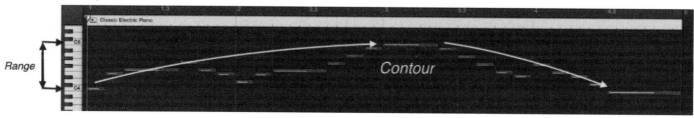

Figure 6.2

The notes of the melody can jump and skip around, and the melody does not have to always end on the note that it started on (Figure 6.3). The variety and possibilities are almost endless.

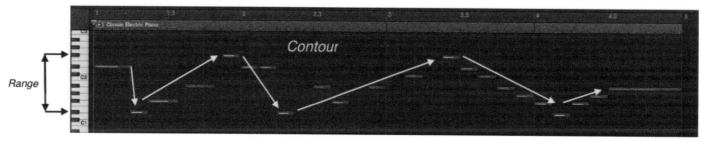

Figure 6.3

The most effective way to create a melody is to experiment and explore playing melodies with a MIDI controller or audio instrument, but if you're not comfortable playing an instrument in real time, the following lesson will guide you through a step entry process for creating a melody.

Melody and Harmony ▶️

This lesson is an extension of the Rhythmic Harmony lesson from Chapter 5. The GarageBand DAW and the harmonic progression in Fig. 5.8 will be used for this lesson.

1. Open a new project in the DAW and create a MIDI track. Enter the chord progression as repeated eighth notes.

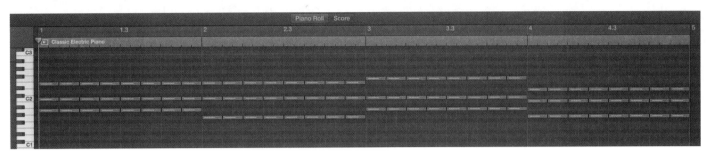

2. Create a new software instrument track in GarageBand. Then hold down the OPTION/ALT key and click and drag the region containing the harmonic progression into the new track and drop it to paste.

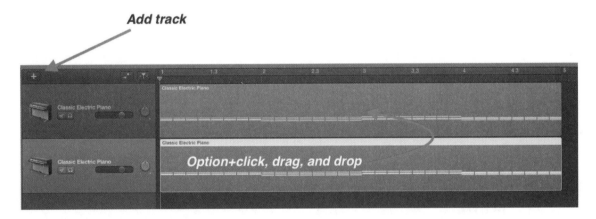

3. Once you begin to create multiple tracks for a song, you must consider the range that you are putting each instrument in. Look at the image of the full-size piano keyboard below. You will want to give each instrument its own area of the keyboard to perform in as much as possible. If all of the instruments or parts of the ensemble are all performing in the same range, the parts will kind of mush all together into a muddled mess of sounds. Fig. 6.4 illustrates some general boundaries for each instrument or voice. Notice that the C notes on the keyboard are numbered to coincide with how the keys are numbered in the DAW.

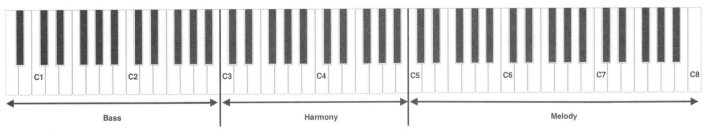

Figure 6.4

To avoid putting the two tracks in this project in the same range, you'll need to move one set of notes up two octaves. Click and drag over all of the notes of one track in the piano roll view to select all of them. Then click and drag up two octaves.

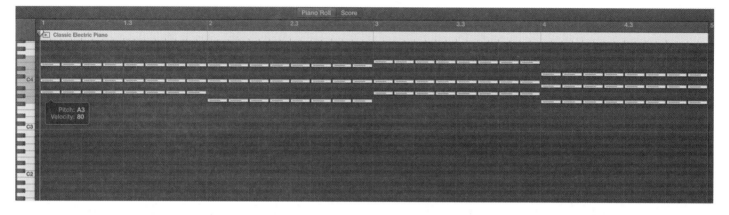

4. Combining the elements of melody and harmony together requires that the two elements work together. This project uses the notes of the harmonic progression to create the melody. It's a process of elimination. The previous image shows all of the notes that you have to choose from to create the melody. Delete the notes that you don't want to use until you have a series of single notes, one after another. You can also delete entire columns of notes to create rhythmic interest and change the length of a single note by clicking and dragging the note's right edge to the desired duration.

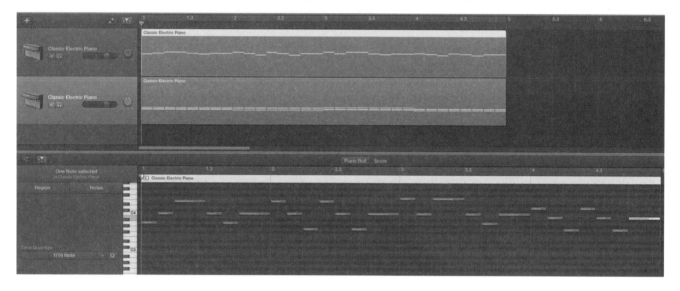

5. Next return to the harmony track and use the procedure from Chapter 5 to create a harmony track with some interesting rhythms that complement the melody.

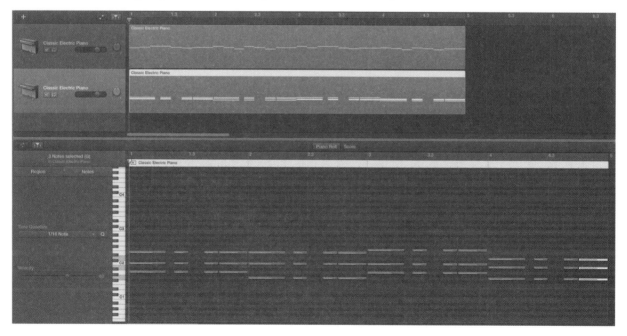

6. Add a drum loop from the loop library or create an original of your own and you are on your way to creating your first original composition!

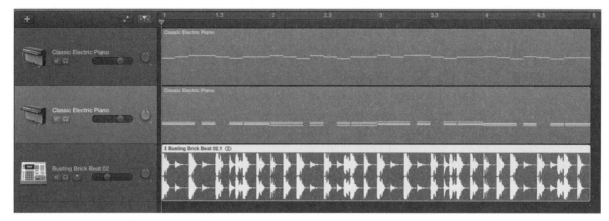

Creating a Bass Line

1. Use the same Melody and Harmony project to continue developing your song. We'll create a bass track to go with the melody, harmony, and drum track. Begin by adding another software track. Use the instrument sample library to select a bass guitar sound that you like.

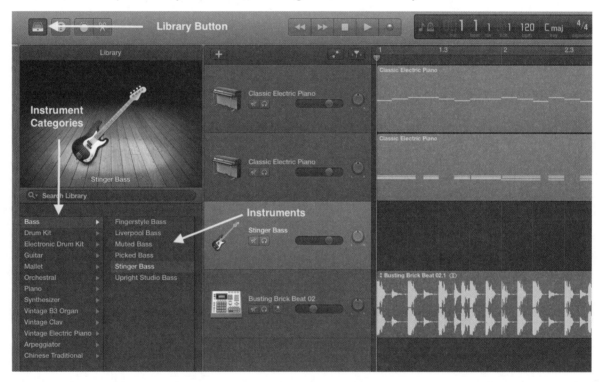

2. It's important to create your bass line in a range below the harmony and melody. If you're not using a larger MIDI controller, you should be able to find an octave control that will allow you to shift the octave down into the bass range. These controls can also be found using a QWERTY keyboard as a MIDI controller.

Octave Shift ➔

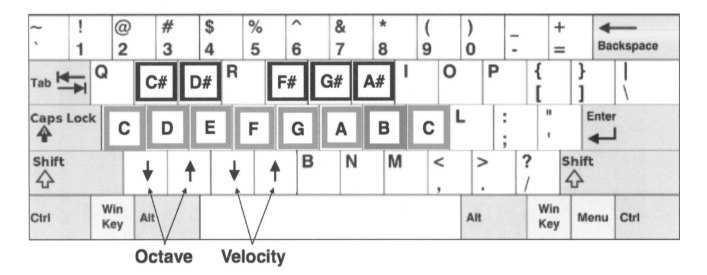

Octave **Velocity**

3. Turn on the cycle bar to loop the music that you have already created. Press the space bar to begin looping the playback of your music.

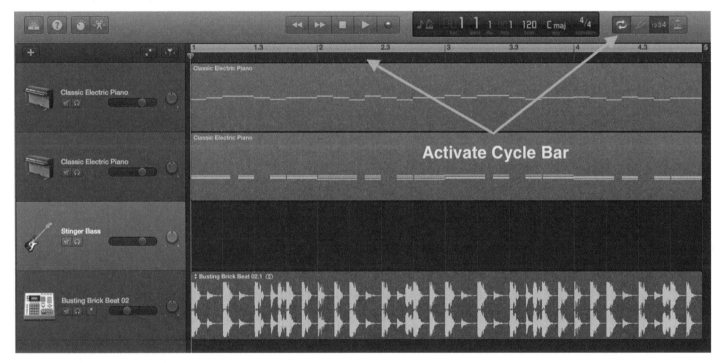

4. Begin improvising a bass line as you are listening to the playback of the music. The image below labels the notes that are in the key of A minor. The capital letters are the "root" notes of the four chords used in the harmony. For measure 1, the root is A; measure 2 is E, measure 3 is F, and measure 4 is G. Until you get more familiar and comfortable improvising a melodic bass line, try playing only the root note in each measure.

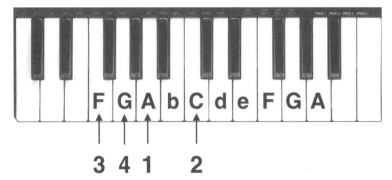

5. Continue improvising and experimenting until you develop some melodic ideas that you like. Set the playhead at the beginning of measure 1 and click the record button when you are ready to record your bass track. You can always delete a track if you mess up, or you can mute a track and add a new one to record several different versions. Remember to use the quantize tool to help correct rhythmic errors and align the tracks.

CHAPTER 7: EXPRESSION

Ultimately, the entire purpose of learning these musical skills is to make music, but why make music? Humans make music because we have something to say, something we need to communicate, or something to express. I often ask my students, "Have you ever felt like you had something to say, but no one was listening?" Or, "Have you ever felt like there was something that you wanted to say, but couldn't figure out quite how to say it?" I think most people can relate to these feelings. Music gives us a way to say something that can compel people to listen who perhaps would not otherwise. Music also gives us an alternate way to express ourselves when words are not enough.

I'm often frustrated with people who tend to think of music performers as artistic and creative types that are somehow inspired by a muse with no need of technical knowledge and skills, while recording engineers and music producers are simply masters of technical knowledge and skills requiring no imagination or creativity. The truth is that the musician spends years developing and honing technical skills and knowledge in order for them to fully utilize their instrument for expression. The recording engineer or music producer must be as equally creative and imaginative as the performer in order to capture the performance and shape it into the final product that will be shared with the audience.

Signal Flow: The Path to Expression

Informed skill mixed with fearless creativity results in true artistry. One fundamental skill lies in understanding how the music is communicated from the performer to the listener. This is referred to as *signal flow* in the home studio or music technology lab. The image below illustrates the most basic level of signal flow (Figure 7.1).

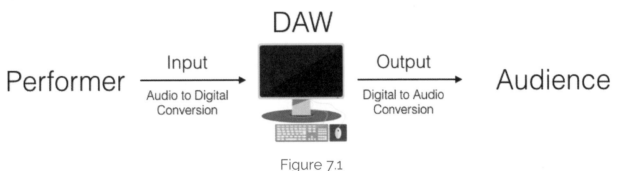

Figure 7.1

There are many things that can be placed in the path between the performer and audience. There are entire books written on various production and mixing techniques. This chapter will focus on some basic concepts to form a solid foundation in future development for the do-it-yourself music producer or student.

Input vs. Output

One of the most common misunderstandings with novice music producers are *input* vs. *output* controls. A great place to start is *pan* vs. *balance* controls. Most people are familiar with balance controls, especially if you've ever experimented with the balance and fade controls of your car stereo speakers. When you turn the balance knob to the left, sound only comes out of the left speakers. Turn the knob to the right, and the sound only comes from the right speakers. Adjusting these controls can make the driver feel as though they are getting sound from all directions (Figure 7.2).

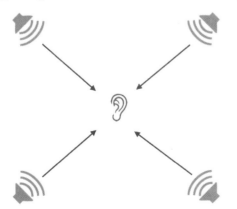

Equal output from all speakers

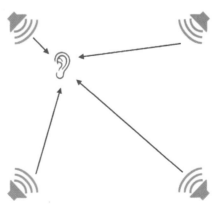

Adjusted outputs from speakers

Figure 7.2

Balance is an output control. When working with audio in the DAW, you have a pan knob. Turning the knob to the left results in the sound coming out of the left speaker or headphone and turning it to the right will result in the sound coming out of the right side. Thinking that balance and pan controls do the same thing is a logical, but incorrect, conclusion. Any control that affects the audio before it enters the DAW or before it leaves the DAW is an *input* control. The pan knob controls how the sound will *leave* the DAW. It cannot be changed once it leaves by the audience or listener. Balance is an output control because it affects the sound after it leaves the DAW. Pan creates a sense of space or surround sound for the audience. A typical pan setup for a rock band would be to pan the drums and vocalist in the center, the bass guitar and rhythm guitar to the left, and the lead guitar and keyboard to the right. When the listener hears this in their headphones and closes their eyes, it sounds as though the drums and vocals are in front of them while the other instrument sounds are coming from the left or right (Figure 7.3).

▶ Panning and Balance

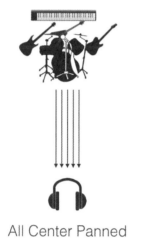

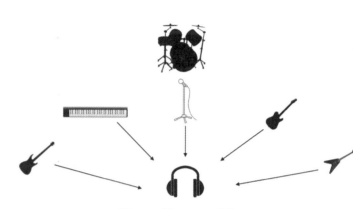

All Center Panned   Stereo/Surround Pan

Figure 7.3

Balance cannot make sound come from the left side if it isn't panned to the left. Turning the balance to the left side would eliminate sounds panned to the right (Figure 7.4).

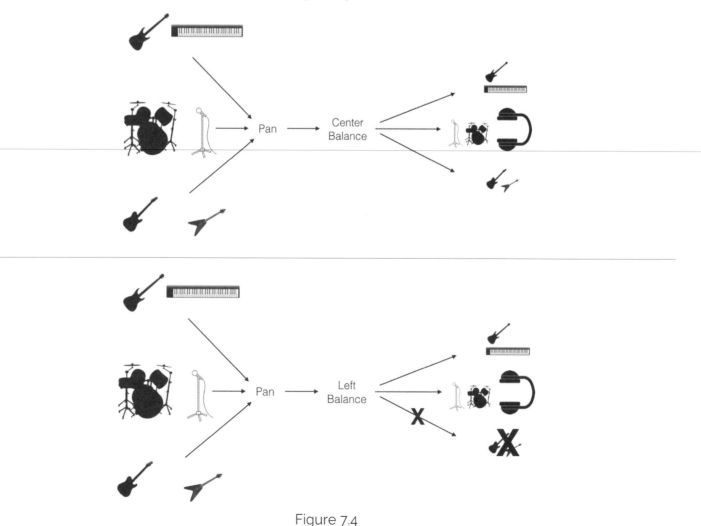

Figure 7.4

▶ Gain and Volume

Gain and *volume* are two other input and output controls that are commonly misunderstood. Gain is an input control that changes the sensitivity of the microphone and the signal that it sends to the DAW. Volume changes the loudness of the sound that comes out of the speakers or headphones to the listener. The novice music producer may turn the gain up and hear the sound get louder and vice versa, leading to a logical conclusion that gain is a volume control, but it isn't. When recording audio into the DAW, you will notice a green, yellow, and red signal meter (Figure 7.5). This signal meter is measuring the strength of the electronic signal coming into the DAW. Green is good. Yellow means caution, and red indicates *clipping*. Clipping occurs when the strength of the audio signal exceeds the capacity of the audio region in the DAW.

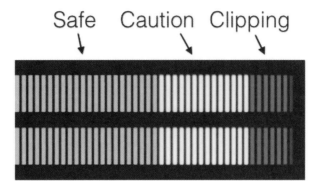

Figure 7.5

The audio signal is literally "clipped" off when it reaches the boundary of the audio region (Figure 7.6).

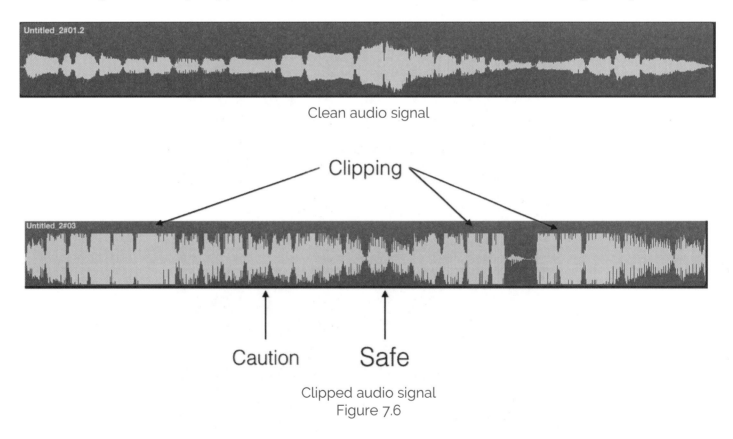

Clean audio signal

Clipped audio signal
Figure 7.6

An audio region with a clipped audio signal will result in a distorted recording of the sound. This distorted sound is similar to turning the volume all the way up until the sound coming from the speakers begins to crack and buzz. This happens because the level of sound output has exceeded the output capacity of the speaker. Turning the volume down eliminates the distortion. If the signal itself is distorted because the gain is set too high, turning the volume down will not fix the problem because the audio signal itself is distorted. Gain is an input control; volume is an output control. Is this beginning to make sense?

Effects

Before the advent and development of digital audio, music producers used a collection of electronic devices to alter and shape sounds to realize the final musical product that they had in their heads. The audio signal had to be routed through each of these devices on the input side to create the desired output. Each machine came with its own set of adjustments, and the order that the signal was routed through the various electronic devices influenced the sound that would eventually be presented to the listener. Music producers and recording engineers had to be highly creative and understand how each device worked to produce the sound that they were "looking" for. Two of the common effects that are used to shape sounds are *equalization* and *compression*.

An equalizer (or *EQ*) is a device that can alter the frequency response of an audio signal. Many home stereo systems and car audio systems come with a very basic EQ that can be used as an output device. Car audio systems will often come with high, mid, and bass controls. Turning the high level up will increase the output of the higher frequencies of the total output signal. This output signal will be all of the audio tracks combined. Turning the bass level up will increase the bass frequencies. If you've ever heard a car stereo system "thumping" out the booming sounds of the bass drum, you were listening to someone who had cranked up the bass level on their EQ.

Equalizers can also be used on the input side of audio and can be used to great effect in shaping and customizing individual tracks in the production (Figure 7.7a). Digital EQ controls can be interfaced in a variety of ways (Figure 7.7b and 7.7c).

EQ
Controls

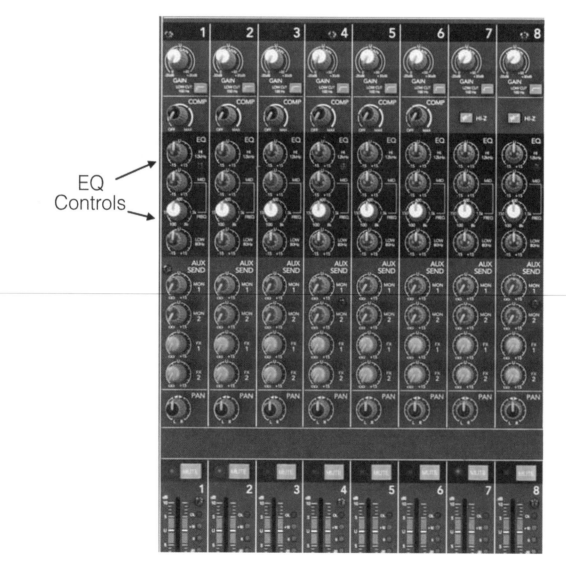

Figure 7.7a

Figure 7.7b

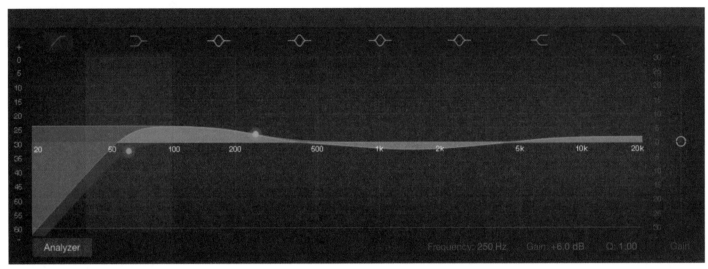

Figure 7.7c

Compression

Compressors are another important effects tool for shaping the sounds of audio signals. A compressor takes the dynamic range of an audio signal and compresses it, making the loudest sounds softer and the softest sounds louder (Figure 7.8).

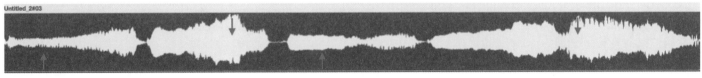

Figure 7.8

Compressors are an effective tool in controlling input volume levels in live performances when levels can change based on microphone placement and the natural variances of human performance. Compressors can also be used to help a track stand out in a mix or to give certain sounds in an audio region more or less articulation.

The order that these and other audio effects are routed through the DAW is also very important. Each effect in a chain will impact the effects that follow, but it's a one-way street. Compressing a signal before equalizing will give you a different result than equalizing the sound before a compressor. There is no right or wrong way to route the signal. Experience and experimentation will bring more nuanced use of these effects into your audio production.

Plug-In Effects ▶

In addition to EQ and compressor effects, there are a wide variety of other effects that can be used to shape and customize audio. Today's modern DAWs have taken what used to be a studio room packed with electronic and analog devices and combined them into a single software package contained on a computer. The digital forms of these audio tools are generically referred to as *virtual studio technologies* (*VSTs*). Before VSTs, the audio signal had to be physically routed through each device using cables that plugged into and out of the devices. These devices became known as *plug-in effects*. Even though the modern DAW eliminates these spider webs of cables, the VST versions are still referred to as plug-in effects. Plug-in effects that can be used with most DAWs fall into four different categories: time-based effects, dynamic effects, modulation effects, and filters.

Time-based effects are created by taking the original audio signal and repeating it in a variety of ways. The most common time-based effects are *reverb* and *delay* (or *echo*) effects. Reverb creates a sense of the space that the sound is happening in. You may notice that you hear sounds differently in the school gym than you do in a classroom. That's because the size and shape of the two spaces are very different. This affects the way that sound moves around in the space before it reaches our ears. Reverb can take a sound that was recorded in a small space, such as a recording booth or your bedroom, and make it sound as though it was recorded in a large concert hall. Delay effects repeat the audio signal in a way that we can hear the repeated sound much like an echo.

Modulation effects are created by taking the audio signal and altering the volume or pitch in a repetitive or pulsing way. Modulation effects are sometimes considered time-based effects because the alteration of the signal can be measured over time. These effects are distinguishable from common time-based effects in that they also alter the amplitude and/or frequency of the signal. Common modulation effects include tremolo, auto-wah, flanger, vibrato, and phaser. There are many different types of modulation effects. Some are better designed for voices and others for instruments. Some work well with both.

Dynamic effects are created by clipping the audio signal to create distortion. The original audio signal should be undistorted when recording because you cannot control or manipulate the level of distortion with clipped audio. Dynamic effects allow control of the distortion and can create some interesting sounds. Common dynamic effects include distortion, fuzz, and overdrive.

Filters affect the sound by increasing or decreasing the different frequencies that are contained in a sound. All sounds are made up of a combination of low, mid, and high frequencies. Even low sounds contain high frequencies, and high sounds contain low frequencies. One thing that makes human voices unique is that all of us have different combinations of low, mid, and high frequencies in the sounds that our vocal cords produce. Filters can bring out or suppress the amount of low, mid, or high frequencies in a sound. Filter effects include equalizers, high pass/cut, mid pass/cut, and low pass/cut combinations.

Plug-in effects can be used alone or in combination with other effects. Music producers spend years learning how to master the art of using plug-in effects and managing signal flow to create the sounds that they want listeners to hear. Exploring and experimenting with plug-in effects and signal flow are important steps in learning how to use them. Most DAWs will include preset effects. *Presets* are combinations of audio effects that have been created for the DAW. You can also save combinations of effects that you create into the presets library for later use. Presets are helpful if you do not have a lot of time to experiment and need to quickly use an effect.

Automation

Another tool that music producers have at their disposal in most DAWs is *automation*. This allows the producer to program the DAW to make adjustments to various parameters automatically over time. While some DAWs like Soundtrap offer a limited number of controls that can be automated (Figure 7.9a), other DAWs offer a wide selection, including tempo and key changes (Figure 7.9b).

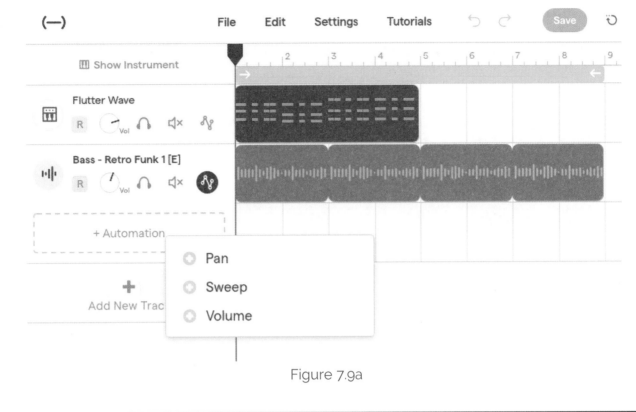

Figure 7.9a

Figure 7.9b

Enabling the automation tool will create a horizontal line within a track that represents time. Clicking on the line will create a small dot or handle that can be moved to make the desired change of the parameter selected. Additional handles can be created to manage the changes over time. In the example below (Figure 7.10), an area of the audio signal is softer than the surrounding audio. The volume control was automated to increase the volume at this point and then gradually return to the original level as the strength of the signal returns. The automation capabilities and user interface of the DAW will vary from platform to platform, but the functionality is the same.

Figure 7.10

Exploring Automation and Effects ▶

Try the following mini-lessons to explore using automation and plug-in effects in your DAW.

Automating Pan

Record a long tone or hum into an audio track of the DAW. Set the pan automation line at the top of the track. Create a handle near the middle of the region and set it at the bottom of the track. Then create a second handle and set it in the middle of the track at the end of the region. Close your eyes and listen to the sound move from left to right before finishing in front of you.

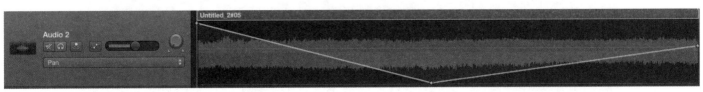

Automating Volume

Record a short script of some sort. Perhaps read a paragraph of an article or book. Add a music loop under the vocal track with both track volumes set at the same level. Notice how the music track covers up the vocal track? Slide the vocal region over so the music track plays first. Now enable automation on the music track and select volume. Create a handle in the music track before the vocal track begins. Create a second handle where the vocal track begins and drag it down to lower the volume of the music track until the vocal track can be clearly heard. This technique is called "ducking"—when the sound of the music "ducks" out of the way so the vocal can be heard.

Exploring Preset Effects

Use the audio track that you recorded into your DAW and experiment with adding preset effects to the vocal track.

Exploring Plug-In Effects

Add a single plug-in effect to the vocal track and then add the same effect to the music track. What difference was there between how the plug-in affected the vocal vs. the music track?

Next, try adding a single plug-in effect to an audio track. Then delete that effect and add a different one. Listen to how the different plug-in effects change the sound in unique ways.

Finally, try adding plug-in effects in combination with one another. Combine a time-based, modulation, dynamic, and filter effect together. Exploration leads to discovery!

CHAPTER 8: TAKING IT ON THE ROAD

Music serves many purposes in our day-to-day lives. Performing or listening to someone else's music can serve both personal and communal needs for rejuvenation, reflection, or celebration. Composing and songwriting is a powerful tool for self-expression, communication, or recreation. Perhaps most importantly, I believe that music is meant to be shared. Digital technology, the internet, wide access to sound and music production tools, and social media have made it easier than ever for people to share their music with friends, community, and the world. Whether you choose to create music as a recreation or as an entrepreneurial endeavor, you have access to the tools that you need to share your music.

Understanding Audio Files

Each DAW available for music production uses its own software program to operate. The working files created when you save a project in a DAW are specific to that DAW. These file formats were not compatible with other DAWs for many years, but that is now beginning to change. It was not possible to create a sample loop in Reason and then export that file into Pro Tools or start a project in Logic Pro and then export the file into Ableton Live for final mixing. It's important to understand what the software of a DAW is doing in the music creation process.

Chapter 2 defined a DAW as an app or software package used to record, edit, and produce audio files. The recording and editing functions of a DAW are process-oriented while the final part of the definition is product-oriented. That last part of the definition is important. The DAW also functions as a sequencer. Google defines the verb form of sequence as "to arrange in a particular order." That is what a DAW does. Every sample, loop, audio or software region, effect, edit, automation, etc., is a piece of information or an instruction that you have programmed into the DAW. The DAW organizes all of these separate pieces of information into essentially a sequence of steps or instructions of what you want to hear, when you want to hear it, and how you want it to be heard.

Though many DAWs are beginning to use a universal file format allowing these files to be shared, a DAW is still required to access the file. This is not a practical way to easily share music with others. In addition, sharing your compositions in this format would allow others to edit or manipulate your composition. The composition should be preserved and presented how the composer or producer created it. This was a problem from the earliest days of the DAW, but there is a solution that most of us are aware of even if not all of us fully understand.

Although the early days of the internet made the transfer of audio files largely impractical, high-speed internet came along in the mid-1990s, and sharing larger amounts of data became more feasible for the consumer market. Consumers began sharing their music files with one another, and a company called Napster tried to capitalize on the new frontier. Lawsuits from the music industry followed, the iPod was born, and when the dust finally settled, the result was that music could now be shared, sold, and stored in a totally digital format. Audio files converted to a digital format still required a great deal of memory, though.

An early audio format was the *WAV* file. This is a "lossless" audio file format, meaning that the file saves all of the captured audio information. The competitive and proprietary relationship between the PC world and Apple computers led Apple to develop their own "lossless" audio file format called the *AIFF* file. WAV and AIFF files are great ways to capture audio files for recording, editing, and producing music in a DAW, but they are not practical for sharing at the consumer level. This led to the development of a file type called a compressed or "lossy" audio file. The concept behind the development of this file format is that there are limitations to the range of human hearing. Certain frequencies extend beyond our hearing capabilities, and when multiple sounds are layered on top of each other, some sounds are masked, meaning that humans do not perceive that the sound is there. Lossy audio files work by splitting the digital audio sound into layers, filtering the layers that fall outside of the range of human perception, and then compressing the remaining information, thus taking up less memory.

The *MP3* was the resulting file format that became the universal standard for compressed audio and was used in the first commercially available digital music players. Apple would soon unveil the iPod and had to have its own version of the compressed, lossy-format audio file called the *AAC*. AAC files do provide a higher-quality audio sound, and it is the format used for music sold in the iTunes store. Other formats have been developed over the years. Several produce better results in sound quality but may not have universal compatibility. There are two open-source (non-patented) formats that are great alternatives. *FLAC* files are very high-quality, lossless audio files that require half the memory of a WAV or AIFF file. FLAC files are not compatible with Apple devices, but apps are available that will store and play FLAC files on an iPhone or iPad. OGG files are an open-source, lossy-format audio file that can be a good alternative to the MP3 or AAC. OGG files also have some compatibility limitations, but it is the file format used by Spotify to stream audio files. Soundtrap by Spotify is one of the few DAWs that provide the option to export audio files in the OGG format.

Those are the options for exporting DAW projects into a shareable audio file. When a DAW project is exported to an audio file, the computer first converts all of the information and instructions that have been sequenced into the DAW through a process called *bouncing* (or *rendering*). Bouncing takes all of the various tracks that have been created with the edits, effects, automation, and other instructions, and compiles everything into a single audio file that can be easily shared and played back. The work that you do in the DAW is like writing out a detailed recipe for a cake. Bouncing is mixing all of the ingredients together and putting it in the oven. The resulting cake is your audio file!

Other Performance Options

In addition to recording and creating music in a DAW, there are other performance opportunities that are commonly pursued in a home studio or music technology lab setting.

Podcasting (iPod + broadcasting = podcasting) has become one of the fastest growing digital media formats. Podcasting originated in the early 2000s as a way to download radio broadcasts or other long-form audio content to the iPod. A podcast is typically a spoken word format featuring a host who either provides commentary about an area of interest or expertise, moderates discussions, or interviews guests. Some podcasts are fictional stories or series, audio journals, or audio versions of video broadcasts. Listeners can subscribe to podcasts via RSS feeds, and podcasters can develop large followings in much the same way as other social media platforms.

Podcasting is not regulated by federal or state laws like TV or radio broadcasters and does not require a license. Content is therefore unlimited. Podcasts can be produced using a DAW and a microphone. The audio is recorded into the DAW. Other audio, such as intro or background music, can be uploaded as well. All of the elements are edited and mixed using the tools of the DAW and then exported as an audio file. Podcasters can then upload the audio files to a webpage or social media site, or submit an application to publish the podcast to a streaming service such as Spotify, Apple Podcasts, Stitcher, Google Music, Amazon, and others. While podcast content is not regulated by federal decency laws, streaming services will typically have content standards and format requirements that must be met.

Learning how to DJ is another option for using music technology as an instrument of music creation and performance. DJ is an abbreviation for "disc jockey." The term was first applied to radio personalities who would select and play records (discs) on radio stations. The early 1970s saw the rise of a different kind of DJ that originated in the Bronx borough of New York City. Block parties became an important part of the social fabric of that community at the time. Someone would bring their stereo equipment and records to play at these parties. They were the DJ. Some DJs gained popularity for not only the selection of music that they played, but the creative ways that they presented the music and engaged with their audience. Artists such as DJ Cool Herc, Grandmaster Flash, and Afrika Bambaataa transformed the record turntable into a performance instrument that was used to combine different songs and transform sections of the records into entirely different musical creations. Their music formed the roots and foundation of hip-hop music. While these early pioneers had to transport crates of equipment and records to their performances, digital technology has created *DJ controllers* that can be contained in a small carrying case along with a laptop or tablet computer (Figure 8.1).

Pioneer DJ SB2

Reloop Mixon 4

Figure 8.1

A successful DJ must consider the audience that they are performing for, curate and select music that will appeal to that audience, and combine and present the music in a highly creative and skillful way. *Remixing* is a performance or recording technique in which the artist takes an original song recorded by someone else and alters the original version by changing, adding to, or deleting certain musical elements of the song. A DJ controller can also be used to combine elements from different songs together to create a new version or remix of the song. DJs can record their performances or remixes using a DAW or the built-in recording capabilities of some DJ controllers. Professional DJs are highly skilled and creative artists.

Creating, Publishing, and Copyright

We are living in a remarkable age for the creative artist and musician. Entrepreneurial access and opportunity for musicians was incredibly limited for most of the 20th century. Musicians simply didn't have access to the tools needed to create recordings, lacked the resources needed to produce records, cassettes, or CDs, and had no advertising budgets to market their products. Record studios and companies controlled the content that was played on the radio or broadcast on TV. Commercially successful musicians often fell victim to unscrupulous lawyers and business practices who crafted contracts that heavily favored the studio over the performers.

Digital technologies have led to the democratization of the music industry. Artists now have most of the tools that they need to produce high-quality recordings in their homes. The portability of digital music files has made CD, cassette, and record players virtually obsolete, eliminating the need to produce physical copies of recordings. Social media puts a powerful marketing tool at your fingertips, and everything that you create belongs to **you**! Your creations have value, and if you choose to monetize your creations, you have a business!

John Snyder is one of the most influential producers of jazz music in the 20th century, having received 32 Grammy nominations and five Grammy awards for recordings he has produced. He's an authority on copyright law as it pertains to recording musicians and is a national advocate and leading educator in music business and entrepreneurship. He writes:

"We are living in the era of the self-sufficient artist. Finally, artists in all of the creative fields are understanding that the flip side of creating is sharing, and sharing implies commerce. And we've found that once they are made aware of the miracle of copyright and the monopoly it provides them, they are as excited as the sailor on the tall mast that sees land first. It's empowering and, done with purpose, it requires just as much creativity and creative problem solving as creating the music."

As soon as you record or create a song or composition by notating it on paper or recording it on a recording device, you become a music publisher, and your creation is protected by federal copyright law. The basis for federal copyright law is found in Article 1, Section 8, clause 8 of the US Constitution:

"The Congress shall have the power to promote the Progress of Science and useful Arts, by securing for limited Times to Authors and Inventors the exclusive Right to their respective Writings and Discoveries."

The Copyright Act of 1976 stipulates that a work must meet three criteria to be protected by copyright: Originality, Works of Authorship, and Fixation. The originality requirement is very broad. Originality does not mean that the content of the work is completely original. It does mean that an existing work cannot simply be copied and then claimed to be original. Works of authorship is also a broad description, but musical works, lyrics, and sound recordings were specified as works of authorship. The last requirement is fixation. This simply means that the work must be recorded in a way that can be shared or communicated with others. This would include notating music using traditional music notation or capturing an audio recording of the work. If you stand in a public park and improvise an original song, that song is not protected. But, as soon as you record it or notate the song, it automatically falls under copyright protection. You do not have to apply or register the work for it to be protected by copyright and you can claim it as copyrighted material. Notated music, music recordings, podcasts, and remixes would all fall under copyright law. If you do not plan to monetize your music, there is no need to register a work for formal copyright. Copyright registration fees range from $50 to $200 depending on a few variables.

Registering a work as a formal copyright does provide some additional advantages for monetized creations. If a work is registered within three months of publication, then you can sue someone for copyright infringement and collect statutory damages and attorney fees. You can still sue someone for infringing on an unregistered work, but you could only collect actual damages such as licensing fees or the profits that were generated through the infringement. It would be difficult to retain a lawyer in this circumstance because you cannot collect attorney fees. Actual damages are difficult to prove and are not likely to cover the legal fees associated with a grievance. Registering the copyright also establishes a public record of the music whose ownership can be transferred to another party. In that way, you could sell the copyright rights to another person or transfer the rights and dictate usage of the copyrighted material to an heir in your will.

This is a very general overview of copyright law. The important takeaway is that, whether you are a do-it-yourself music producer, podcaster, DJ, or a student creating music in a music technology course, the content that you create belongs to you, has value, and has legal protections under federal law. Visit *copyright.gov* for more information.

Sharing and Distributing

If you have no desire to monetize your music, there are certainly many options available for you to share your music. You could create a website to upload your music for sharing, post links to your website, or post audio files and share via social media. SoundCloud is a social media website that was created for people to upload and share their music with others or to discover music by independent artists.

If you want to monetize your music and earn money, then you will likely need a *music distributor*. A distributor not only provides access to your music for a wider audience, but it will also collect and manage revenue generated from your music. Pandora, Apple Music, Spotify, Amazon Prime Music, Google Play, and YouTube Music are not distributors. They are *music streaming services*. Tencent is a music streaming service operating in the quickly growing Chinese market. A music distributor will get your music distributed to all or some of these streaming services and collect royalties earned when your music is streamed to return to you.

There are many music distribution companies available that will distribute your music to the major streaming services. Some of them include: DistroKid, CD Baby, TuneCore, Landr, ReverbNation, Amuse, AWAL, and Record Union. I do not endorse these companies but share them as some of the more popular distributors in the market. It pays (literally) to do your research on the services that they offer and their fee structure.

SoundCloud was an early platform for musicians to share and discover music with other independent artists. SoundCloud has added a distribution option for Premium users to get their music published on the major streaming platforms in addition to selling their music in SoundCloud. Another similar option is BandCamp. BandCamp provides a platform for artists to sell their music directly to their audience without having to share the revenue with distributors or streaming services. It's kind of like eBay for music! The exciting part is that you are in control of your music.

Becoming a skilled and artistic music creator does not just happen. Musicians do not sit around and wait for a visit from a muse or divine inspiration. Skill and artistry develop over time. You will make a lot—and I mean *a lot*—of bad music before you begin to make music that isn't *too* bad. Keep working and it becomes pretty good. Before you know it, other people will start to notice and want to listen. This is true for teachers also. Most music teachers are trained in the classical and formal art of music-making but may have very little experience with music technology. The role of any music teacher is to teach students how to use the instrument that they have to make music. That may be a trumpet, clarinet, voice, violin, cello, or DAW. Teach students how to make music—not only how to use the computer or app. We do not teach a student how to play a saxophone just for the sake of being able to operate a saxophone. Music and creativity are the foundations upon which all of the other skills and knowledge are built.

AFTERWORD: WHAT IS CREATIVITY AND CAN IT BE TAUGHT?

As a noun, Merriam-Webster defines *creativity* as "the ability to create." That sounds a bit mundane. The verb form *create* is defined as "to bring into existence." Now that's quite a leap from the "ho-hum" into the realm of the omnipotent! I think my favorite is the adjective form, *creative*, which is defined as "marked by the ability or power to create." That seems to be a good middle ground. Being creative may be a super-power, but it does not make you a god!

I believe that this extraordinary variation in the gravity of these definitions illustrates the challenge that many of us have with the idea of teaching someone to be creative. Other words that I can think of mostly stay in the same lane as they move from a verb to noun to an adjective: act, action, activity; produce, pro-duction, productivity; etc. But *create* seems to be different. Culturally and historically, we associate creativity with the realm of the arts. Creative geniuses, such as da Vinci, Picasso, Beethoven, and Stravinsky, are placed upon pedestals as great artists. Their creations are only displayed or performed in formal museums or concert halls that we must enter into from the casual environment of everyday existence. Even when we dig into the creative underground of street artists like Plastic Jesus and Banksy, or musicians like Bob Marley, John Lennon, and Jimi Hendrix, we tend to view them as almost mythological creative beings. When we elevate creativity into this preternatural status, it's no wonder that we mere mortals become so intimidated at the prospect of teaching creativity.

It's also important to recognize that there are many examples of creative genius outside of the world of the arts. There is perhaps no greater example of this than Isaac Newton. Newton used his imagination to create an abstract test (equation) that could explain a natural phenomenon that was untestable through physical means. Some may argue that Newton didn't create anything. He was simply explaining what made the apple fall from the tree. I would counter that he was able to see what could not be seen and was able to express that in a way that the world could see. I believe this is not dissimilar to the musician who hears what has yet to be heard and is able to express these sounds in a way that the world can hear also. Were Steve Jobs and Steve Wozniak being creative when they were developing what would become the world's most successful computer company? Creativity, innovation, invention, imagination—all of these terms are synonymous and span the range of human endeavor from science to art.

What then is the best definition? Returning to our friends Merriam and Webster, I believe the most accurate definition is the transitive verb form: "to produce through imaginative skill." Can these imaginative skills be taught? Yes, but we need to reconsider and reevaluate our perspective of how we value creativity.

CREATIVE vs. Creative vs. creative

The first step in demystifying the idea of creative genius is to recognize the creativity that is happening within and around us all of the time. Culturally, we're conditioned to recognize and value what has been described by psychologists, such as Dean Keith Simonton, James Kaufman, and Ronald Beghetto, as "Big-C creativity." "Big-C creativity consists of clear-cut, eminent creative contributions" (Kaufman and Beghetto, 2009). Big-C creativity is easy to identify: the Mona Lisa, Beethoven's 9th Symphony, Moog's synthesizer, winning a Pulitzer Prize, Edison's lightbulb, etc. These are tremendous achievements in human creativity, but these types of creative products represent only the very tip of the iceberg of creativity. The idea of setting out to teach creativity is intimidating and overwhelming when this is the standard that we believe must be reached.

Perhaps now would be a good time to revisit Merriam-Webster's definition of "creative": *the ability to create*. That's simple and succinct. We *all* have the ability to create, and we are all in a creative state of mind most of the time. Because we have been so programmed to focus and value the "Big-C" creations, we simply miss or, at least, devalue the creative actions that we take every day. Say, for example, you're preparing dinner one evening. You begin going through your recipe to prepare the dish and realize that you're missing an ingredient. That's when your creative mind kicks in and begins formulating different options. The recipe says to add allspice, but you're out of allspice. Maybe cumin would work instead? And then maybe add a little paprika? Voila! That's what Kaufman and Beghetto describe as "little-c" creativity. "Too much of a focus on Big-C leads to the ideas that only certain people can be creative, the only creativity that matters is that of the Big-C kind" (Kaufman and Beghetto, 2009). A critical concept to understand and accept if we are going to teach creativity is that *everyone* is creative.

Kaufman and Beghetto took the concept of "Big-C" and "little-c" creativity a step further with another level of creativity that they describe as "mini-c" creativity (Kaufman and Beghetto, 2007). They define mini-c creativity as "the novel and personally meaningful interpretation of experiences, actions, and events." This form of creativity is particularly important to the teacher because it's the type that takes place in the process of learning something new. The key part of "mini-c" is the "personally meaningful interpretation" of what the students are being taught. Students must be encouraged to explore the tools and resources we give them to create music. Through this process of exploration, they're going to discover sounds, techniques, and unique combinations of processes that they will be able to use in creating music. These are "mini-c" moments. This type of learning is sometimes referred to as *tacit learning*. Tacit learning is difficult to observe and measure, and we often miss the value of it because of this, but it's nevertheless critical in the process of developing creativity. Dr. Adam Patrick Bell writes in his book *Dawn of the DAW*, "For the music educator, it is critical to recognize that what is of utmost importance is to create contexts in which tacit learning can occur." The role of the teacher in this context is not to impart knowledge to the student but to serve as a facilitator of learning or a guide for the student as they explore the tools of music creation.

Educational institutions do a very effective job of conditioning the natural curiosity and creativity out of students by the age of eight or nine. Students learn that the secret to success in school is to get the right answer as quickly as possible and to avoid wrong answers. They learn to value *answers* instead of *knowledge*. Those things are easier to quantify and generate data from in the educational world of accountability and assessment under which the educational system has functioned since the early 2000s.

Creativity is not a skill that can be taught through a step-by-step process, but rather it's an ability that should be nurtured and developed over time. Mistakes are not only necessary; they're a valuable part of learning. Possessing knowledge and skill results in confidence. It's important for the teacher to encourage and instill confidence until students are able to develop that knowledge and skill. I stress to beginning students that I am assessing them on *process* not *product*. They have to understand that the music they create is not going to sound like their favorite music on the radio right away, and that is OK! Creating any type of original work is a very personal process. No one wants to draw a picture and then have their friends laugh about how bad it is. Cultivate an environment where students feel safe and empowered to make mistakes. Assess the process and cultivate the product. Most great musicians began as bad, inexperienced musicians. They became great because they were not deterred by the bad sounds that first came out of their instruments. The reality is that all great monuments of human creativity started as something very small: an idea.

APPENDIX A
Song Project Unit for Summative Assessment

The students will create a recording of a song from start to finish. They are responsible for creating, composing, and producing all aspects of the song, including the lyrics, music, recording, final mix, and production. This project is the first summative assessment that I use with my beginning music technology students. The project is collaborative, with students working in groups of three or four. There's a lesson plan for each week, but the full project generally takes three to four weeks to complete. Over the course of the project, most of the NAfME standards (National Association for Music Education) for music technology will be addressed. There are four assessment points in the project. The first three are formative in nature, with the final assessment being a final summative grade. The lesson plans for each phase of the project are available as a downloadable PDF using the link and access code on page 1 of this book.

Overview

Week 1: Writing Lyrics

Week 2: Creating Music Tracks

Week 3: Recording Vocals

Week 4: Final Mixing, Editing, Effects, and Production

Outline

(Based on four classes per week with 46-minute class periods)

1. Week One - Lyrics
    a) Day 1: Intro to lyric writing lesson
    b) Day 2-3: Brainstorming and lyric writing
    c) Day 4: Submit final lyrics for song

2. Week Two - Music
    a) Day 1: Intro to creating/composing music
    b) Day 2-3: Improvising, selecting, analyzing, and refining
    c) Day 4: Submit final music tracks

3. Week Three - Recording Vocals
    a) Day 1: Intro to recording (mics, input/output controls, methods)
    b) Day 2-3: Groups rotate between two recording stations
    c) Day 4: Begin work on mixing, editing, and effects

4. Week Four - Final Mix and Production
    a) Day 1: Mix and production feedback
    b) Day 2-3: Final mix and production
    c) Day 4: Presentation of student work

Lyric Writing Worksheet

Title of song (hook):

Chorus   **Rhyming words**

_____

_____

- -

_____

_____

Verse 1

_____

_____

- -

_____

_____

Verse 2

_____

_____

- -

_____

_____

Bridge

_____

_____

- -

_____

_____

Name: _____

Song Project Assessment Rubric

	5	4	3	2	1
Lyrics	Message of song is clearly expressed in the lyrics. Lyrics are structured to match the form with a clear and creative rhyme scheme.	Message of song is clearly expressed in the lyrics. Lyrics are structured to mostly match the form with mostly clear and creative rhyme scheme.	Message of song is somewhat ambiguous in the lyrics. The lyrics are not always structured to match the form, not always using clear or creative rhyme schemes.	Message of song is ambiguous in the lyrics. The lyrics are rarely structured to match the form with little evidence of a rhyme scheme.	No message is apparent in the lyrics. There is no evidence of structure of rhyme scheme with the lyrics.
Music Tracks	Musical style and instrumentation are very effective in enhancing the mood, context, and message of the song, utilizing correct form and phrasing.	Musical style and instrumentation are effective in enhancing the mood, context, and message of the song, utilizing correct form and phrasing.	Musical style and instrumentation are somewhat effective in enhancing the mood, context, and message of the song, with minimal errors in form and phrasing.	Musical style and instrumentation are rarely effective in enhancing the mood, context, and message of the song, with obvious errors in form and phrasing.	Musical style and instrumentation has no effect in enhancing the mood, context, and message of the song, with no evidence of form or phrasing.
Vocal Performance & Recording	Vocal performance shows clear evidence of preparation with no errors. Vocal recording captures a high level of expressive performance.	Vocal performance shows evidence of preparation with almost no errors. Vocal recording captures a moderate level of expressive performance.	Vocal performance shows some evidence of preparation with minor errors. Vocal recording captures a minimal level of expressive performance.	Vocal performance shows almost no evidence of preparation with significant errors. Vocal recording captures almost no expressive performance.	Vocal performance shows no evidence of preparation with significant errors throughout. Vocal recording captures no expressive performance.
Editing, Mixing & Effects	Editing, mixing, and effects are continuously used in highly creative ways to enhance the message and expression of the song.	Editing, mixing, and effects are often used in highly creative ways to enhance the message and expression of the song.	Editing, mixing, and effects are sometimes used in creative ways to enhance the message and expression of the song.	Editing, mixing, and effects are rarely used in creative ways to enhance the message and expression of the song.	Editing, mixing, and effects are never used in creative ways to enhance the message and expression of the song.
Planning & Project Management	Project planning and management were highly effective, allowing ample time for reflection, revision, and collection of feedback.	Project planning and management were effective, allowing time for reflection, revision, and collection of feedback.	Project planning and management allowed some time for reflection, revision, and collection of feedback.	Project planning and management allowed only limited time for reflection, revision, and some collection of feedback.	Project planning and management allowed no time for reflection, revision, and collection of feedback.

Final Score: _____

Other Comments:

APPENDIX B

Chord Progression Flow Chart
Major Keys

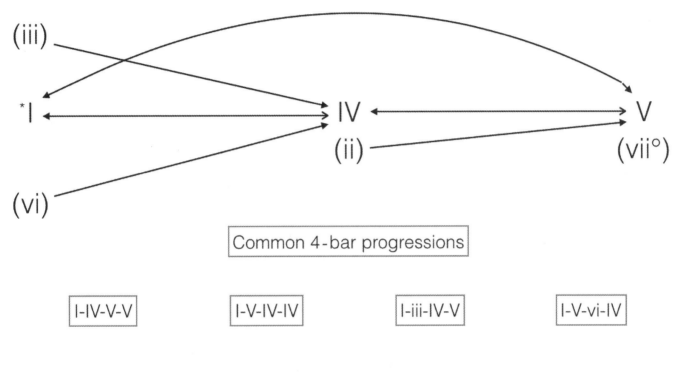

Common 4-bar progressions

| I-IV-V-V | I-V-IV-IV | I-iii-IV-V | I-V-vi-IV |

Chord Progression Flow Chart
Minor Keys

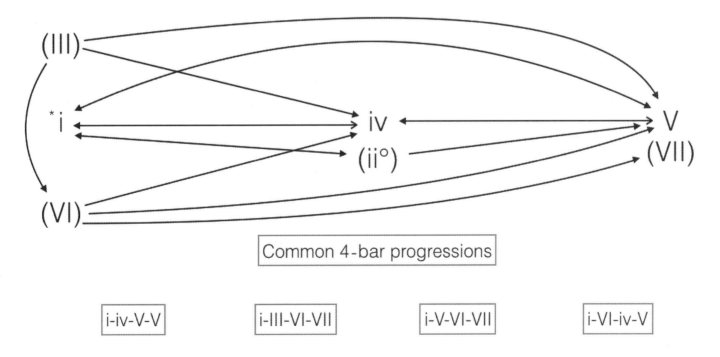

Common 4-bar progressions

| i-iv-V-V | i-III-VI-VII | i-V-VI-VII | i-VI-iv-V |

* I or i can go anywhere.

COMPANY INDEX

Akai	https://www.akaipro.com
Alesis	https://www.alesis.com
Amuse	https://www.amuse.io
Aston Microphones	https://www.astonmics.com
Audio Technica	https://www.audio-technica.com
Avid-Pro Tools	https://www.avid.com/pro-tools
AWAL	https://www.awal.com
BandCamp	https://bandcamp.com
Blue Microphones	https://www.bluedesigns.com
CD Baby	https://cdbaby.com
Distrokid	https://distrokid.com
GarageBand	https://www.apple.com/mac/garageband
Jamstick	https://jamstik.com
Korg	https://www.korgusa.com
Landr	https://www.landr.com
M-Audio	https://www.m-audio.com
Native Instruments	https://www.native-instruments.com
Novation	https://novationmusic.com
On Stage Stands	https://on-stage.com
Pioneer DJ	https://www.pioneerdj.com
Presonus	https://www.presonus.com
Primacoustic	https://www.primacoustic.com
Reason Studios	https://www.reasonstudios.com
Record Union	https://www.recordunion.com
Reloop	https://www.reloop.com
Reverb Nation	https://www.reverbnation.com
Roland	https://www.roland.com
Samson	http://www.samsontech.com
sE Electronics	https://www.seelectronics.com
Shure	https://www.shure.com
SoundCloud	https://soundcloud.com
Soundtrap by Spotify	https://www.soundtrap.com
Steinberg	https://www.steinberg.net
Tune Core	https://www.tunecore.com
Yamaha Music	https://usa.yamaha.com/products/musical_instruments
Zoom	https://www.zoomcorp.com

*PHOTO CREDITS

Figure 2.1   By Brandon Daniel derivative work: Clusternote (talk) - Roland_TR-808_&_909.jpg, CC BY-SA 2.0, https://commons.wikimedia.org/w/index.php?curid=33527250

Figure 2.2   Mojo Synths, derivative work: E-mu Emulator II+.png: Clusternote derivative work: This file was derived from: E-mu Emulator II+.jpg; E-mu Emulator II+.png, CC BY-SA 3.0, https://commons.wikimedia.org/w/index.php?curid=48702175

Figure 2.3   By Lanisha Cole - Own work, CC BY-SA 4.0, https://commons.wikimedia.org/w/index.php?curid=80758057

Figure 2.15   Patrick Woodward / CC BY (https://creativecommons.org/licenses/by/2.0)

Figure 2.16   ArtBrom / CC BY-SA (https://creativecommons.org/licenses/by-sa/2.0)

Figure 2.17   By Amin Asbaghipour: https://www.pexels.com/@llane-a?utm_content=attributionCopyText&utm_medium=referral&utm_source=pexels

*All other images in this publication were either created by the author or used under free use permission with no requirement of attribution.

BIBLIOGRAPHY

"8 of the Best Digital Music Distribution Companies (2020)." *Sundown Sessions Studio*, 26 Mar. 2020, sundownsessionsstudio.com/best-digital-music-distribution-companies/.

Bell, Adam Patrick. *Dawn of the DAW: The Studio as Musical Instrument*. Oxford University Press, 2018.

"Interactive Constitution: The National Constitution Center." *Interactive Constitution | The National Constitution Center*, constitutioncenter.org/interactive-constitution.

Jones, Heath, and John Snyder. "Producing, Copyright & Entrepreneurship." *MuTechTeacherTalk*, Heath Jones, June 2019, www.mutechteachernet.com/mutechteachertalk/2019/10/13/episode-9-producing-copyright-amp-entrepreneurship-with-john-snyder. Accessed 2020.

Kaufman, James and Beghetto, Ronald. (2009). Beyond Big and Little: The Four C Model of Creativity. Review of General Psychology - REV GEN PSYCHOL. 13. 10.1037/a0013688.

Levine, Mike. "The History of the DAW." *Yamaha Music*, 1 May 2019, hub.yamaha.com/the-history-of-the-daw/.

MacDonald, Jay. "Grammy-Winning Producer John Snyder on the Business of Music." *CreditCards.com*, 1 Apr. 2019, www.creditcards.com/credit-card-news/grammy_winning-producer-john_snyder-business_of_music-1264/.

MasterClass. "What Is Verse-Chorus Form? Examples of Verse-Chorus Form in Pop, Folk, and Hip-Hop - 2020." *MasterClass*, MasterClass, 7 Oct. 2019, www.masterclass.com/articles/what-is-verse-chorus-form-examples-of-verse-chorus-form-in-pop-folk-and-hip-hop.

Mlynczak, John. *Professional Development*. Mar. 2020, johnmlynczak.com/presentations.

Nichols, Phillip. "Downloadable Charts to Understand Audio Signal Flow in a DAW." *IZotope*, 7 July 2018, www.izotope.com/en/learn/understanding-audio-signal-flow-in-a-daw.html.

Rose, Joel, and Jacob Ganz. "The MP3: A History of Innovation and Betrayal." *NPR*, NPR, 23 Mar. 2011, www.npr.org/sections/therecord/2011/03/23/134622940/the-mp3-a-history-of-innovation-and-betrayal.

Strong, Maria. "U.S. Copyright Office." *Copyright*, U.S. Copyright Office, www.copyright.gov/.

Tysver, Daniel A. "BitLaw." *Obtaining Copyright Protection (BitLaw)*, 2019, www.bitlaw.com/copyright/obtaining.html.

Watson, Stephanie. "How Podcasting Works." *HowStuffWorks*, HowStuffWorks, 26 Mar. 2005, computer.howstuffworks.com/internet/basics/podcasting1.htm.

ABOUT THE AUTHOR

Heath Jones currently teaches Music Technology at McConnell Middle School for Gwinnett County Public Schools in Lawrenceville, GA. He serves as the Lead Teacher for Middle Grades Music Technology for Gwinnett County Public Schools and is the Music Technology Chair for the Georgia Music Educators Association. He organized the first ever GMEA Music Technology Student Showcase in 2020 to recognize the most outstanding music technology students and their teachers in the state.

Heath began his career as a high school band director and has 23 years of teaching experience. His high school bands in Georgia, South Carolina, and Tennessee consistently performed at a high level in all areas of the wind band activity and were invited performers at regional and state level conferences. Since transitioning to teaching music technology, he has continued to be involved in the marching arts activity as a drill designer and consultant for several high school bands and winter guards in the Atlanta area.

As part of his development as a music technology teacher, he's been a part of working committees for the Gwinnett County Public Schools and the Georgia Department of Education in developing curriculum, performance standards, and assessments at both the state and local level. He is in demand as a guest lecturer, having presented sessions at the NAfME National Conference, the Midwest International Band and Orchestra Clinic, and several state-level conferences on topics of music technology and curriculum. He's also a Google Level 1 Certified Educator, Apple Educator, and a certified Soundtrap and Noteflight Educator. Heath is the creator of *www.mutechteachernet.com*, which supports and encourages an international audience of music technology educators and enthusiasts. He's passionate in his work to support and encourage his own students while advocating for the continued growth of music technology programs in his state, region, and country. Heath lives in Dacula, GA with his wife, Jeanine, and their two children, William and Abigail.

Connect with Heath on Facebook, Instagram, and YouTube @mutechteahernet and on Twitter @mutechteachnet.